"Not all driving forces within a leader are positive. Becoming a strong leader requires not only the cultivation of God-given gifts, but the ability to overcome negative factors. I recommend *Overcoming the Dark Side of Leadership* . . . to anyone striving to overcome obstacles in order to become a more effective leader."

John Maxwell, founder, Injoy

"Gary and Sam give leaders permission to confront the darkest battles within in order to serve others in life-transforming ways. For all who are bold enough to embark on this courageous journey, redemption, restoration, and renewal will be your rewards."

Dr. Stephen A. Macchia, founder and president, Leadership Transformations, Inc.; director, Pierce Center, Gordon-Conwell Theological Seminary; author, *Becoming a Healthy Team*

"One of the most important qualities an effective leader must possess is often the most lacking: self-awareness. Effective leaders are acutely self-aware, knowing not only their strengths but also their weaknesses—the dark side of those strengths. And without this self-awareness, many leaders crash and burn without realizing their full potential for the kingdom of God. In *Overcoming the Dark Side of Leadership*, Gary McIntosh and Sam Rima have done a masterful job of helping leaders avoid the pitfalls that have consumed far too many leaders. This is a must-read for any leader who is serious about taking his or her leadership to the next level."

Dr. Albert L. Winseman, global practice leader for faith communities, The Gallup Organization; author, *Growing an Engaged Church: How to Stop "Doing Church" and Start Being the Church Again*

"Every leader has a 'shadow' side, like the dark side of the moon—areas that are disguised, or perhaps explored but unrecognized. I am convinced that our leadership will be stronger and the dangers of collapse lesser if we become aware of these dark areas and bring them into the light early."

Leighton Ford, president, Leighton Ford Ministries

"There is no question in my mind of the practicality, relevancy, and usefulness of this book. I have a difficult time thinking who would not be helped by reading it; seminarians, pastors, and denominational and parachurch leaders would all benefit. . . . Anyone who is serious about being a good leader will be helped by this book."

Robert Ricker, former president, Baptist General Conference

"This book will help you gain the insights necessary to protect yourself from significant failure."

Rob Angel, creator of Pictionary

OVERCOMING THE
DARK SIDE
OF LEADERSHIP

Other books by Gary L. McIntosh

Beyond the First Visit
Biblical Church Growth
Church That Works
Creating Community
The Exodus Principle
One Church, Four Generations
Staff Your Church for Growth

Other books by Samuel D. Rima

Leading from the Inside Out

OVERCOMING THE
DARK SIDE
OF LEADERSHIP

How to Become an Effective Leader
by Confronting Potential Failures

REVISED EDITION

Gary L. McIntosh
Samuel D. Rima

BakerBooks
Grand Rapids, Michigan

© 1997, 2007 by Gary L. McIntosh and Samuel D. Rima

Published by Baker Books
a division of Baker Publishing Group
P.O. Box 6287, Grand Rapids, MI 49516-6287
www.bakerbooks.com

Second printing, October 2008

Printed in the United States of America

Library of Congress Cataloging-in-Publication Data
McIntosh, Gary, 1947–
    Overcoming the dark side of leadership : how to become an effective leader by confronting potential failures / Gary L. McIntosh, Samuel D. Rima.— Rev. ed.
        p.   cm.
    Includes bibliographical references (p.   ).
    ISBN 10: 0-8010-6835-5 (pbk.)
    ISBN 978-0-8010-6835-5 (pbk.)
    1. Christian leadership—Psychology. I. Rima, Samuel D. II. Title.
BV652.1.M394 2007
253—dc22   2007022636

Unless otherwise indicated, Scripture is taken from the New American Standard Bible®, Copyright © 1960, 1962, 1963, 1968, 1971, 1972, 1973, 1975, 1977, 1995 by The Lockman Foundation. Used by permission.

Scripture marked NRSV is taken from the New Revised Standard Version of the Bible, copyright 1989, Division of Christian Education of the National Council of the Churches of Christ in the United States of America. Used by permission. All rights reserved.

Sam: I dedicate this book to my wife, Sue. Because of her Christlike character and incredible love for me I have been better able to deal with the shadow side of my character. She is my best friend and my greatest asset in ministry and life. She has enabled me to go places and accomplish goals that would have been impossible without her.

I also dedicate this book to Dr. Greg Bourgond, a friend and mentor who encourages and motivates me and many others to always live and lead in God's strength and to his honor.

Gary: I dedicate this book to the members of Grace Baptist Church in San Bernardino, California, who patiently endured my struggle with the dark side and lovingly supported me through it all (1976–1983). May every young pastor be blessed by a similar, caring congregation.

CONTENTS

PREFACE

The proliferation of significant leadership failures within the Christian church and various other Christian organizations during the final two decades of the twentieth century has been without doubt one of the most serious threats to the continued credibility and viability of Christianity in an increasingly secular and skeptical American culture. It is not uncommon to hear on an almost monthly basis of yet another failure within some segment of the Christian leadership community. Unfortunately it seems that it is very often those leaders occupying highly visible and influential positions who are the victims of these failures.

In light of this increase in failures among Christian leaders, or at least our increased awareness of them, something must be done to educate present and future leaders as to the causes, results, and potential prevention of these failures. Sadly, very little training is given in this area at the seminary and graduate school level to help future leaders diagnose and address personal issues that may plague them in their exercise of leadership. It is our prayer that this book will assist in doing so.

The Seeds for This Study

Sam's initial interest in the dark side of leadership was kindled during his seminary days as he watched the ministry empire of Jim Bakker begin to crumble on national television. Watching in amazement as the Bakkers broadcast desperate and convoluted explanations of their sexual exploits, drug addictions, clandestine payoffs, and financial failures while in leadership at PTL, Sam wondered how a Christian leader like Jim Bakker could have fallen so far and committed such nefarious acts. It was a wake-up call of sorts. During the aftermath of the PTL debacle, additional reports of moral failure involving Jimmy Swaggart and his fellow evangelist Marvin Gorman began to reveal how widespread such dalliances with the dark side were among Christian leadership ranks.

Gary's concern for the dark side of leadership gained focus shortly after he became director of the Doctor of Ministry program at Talbot School of Theology in the fall of 1986. Within a few short years he watched in frustration and pain as his two most popular adjunct professors—Gordon MacDonald and Frank Tillapaugh—disclosed moral failures.

What caused gifted leaders such as Frank Tillapaugh, Gordon MacDonald, Jim Bakker, Jimmy Swaggart, and others to fail so dramatically in spite of their obvious love for God and passion for his church? One would think that people in such high-profile positions would take special care to maintain a reputation above reproach. It almost seemed as if these leaders were driven to experience failure in equal proportion to their success.

We began informally to explore the background of these leaders in an effort to learn what, if anything, was the common thread in their failures. We were desperate to learn how we could protect ourselves from such humiliating failure in the future and help others to avoid similar defeats.

We observed that in spite of the waves of moral failure lapping the shores of the Christian world at that time, few people preparing for leadership received instruction or other assistance on this issue. In some schools it seemed to be a topic that was almost purposely neglected. The failure of Christian leaders was like a family secret no one wanted to talk about. This was especially true when news of the downfall of evangelical leaders of national renown hit the media.

Another motivating factor in the inception of this book was our own personal struggles with the dark side. Sam discovered that an unhealthy compulsion to succeed led to a period of depression and burnout. What was it that drove him to work fourteen-hour days and still feel like a slacker? Why did he constantly feel that others disapproved of his leadership? Gary experienced a similar drivenness that led to people's resisting his leadership. The ultimate frustrations spilled over into his family life. What made him so tired that he would fall asleep while trying to study for next Sunday's message? Why did he find his vision failing for a ministry and people he honestly loved? These were issues we knew we must explore if we were to continue to be useful to God in his kingdom work.

These experiences led us to engage in a detailed study of leadership failures, their causes, and potential prevention. Our research focused on the reading of many biographies, psychological works, and books on spiritual formation and leadership, as well as personal conversations and interviews with leaders from various walks of life.

It was during this research that it became clear that a paradox of sorts existed in the lives of most of the leaders who had experienced significant failures: the personal insecurities, feelings of inferiority, and need for parental approval (among other dysfunctions) that compelled these people to become successful leaders were very often the same issues that precipitated their failure. This paradox can be seen in the lives of such varied leaders as Adolf Hitler, General Douglas MacArthur, Richard Nixon, and Senator Gary Hart, to name only a few. It can also be seen in the lives of some of the leaders in the Bible.

We then needed to find a way to help leaders recognize and deal with the dark side in themselves. The result was a strategy that leaders, armed with new understanding about themselves, can implement that may enable them to triumph over their dark side and avoid significant failure in their exercise of leadership.

The Basic Assumptions of the Book

As in all works, there are numerous assumptions foundational to the development of this book and the reader's understanding of the material presented. These are assumptions derived from our study of various subject matters, including our own personal experiences, a substantial array of literature on the subjects of leadership and personal dysfunction, and observation and conversations with those involved in the leadership of churches and numerous Christian organizations. Briefly, it is assumed:

1. Every leader suffers from some degree of personal dysfunction varying from extremely mild to extremely acute.
2. Personal dysfunction, in one form or another, can often serve as the driving force behind an individual's desire to achieve success as a leader.
3. Many leaders are not aware of the dark side of their personalities and the personal dysfunctions that drive them.
4. The personal characteristics that drive individuals to succeed and lead often have a shadow side that can cripple them once they become leaders and very often causes significant failure. This dynamic is what has been labeled in this book the "paradox of personal dysfunction in leadership."
5. Learning about their own dark side and the dysfunctions that have created it can enable leaders to address those areas and prevent, or at least mitigate, the potential negative effects to their exercise of leadership.

14

6. Scripture has much to say about the dark side of human personality and the motivations that drive us to achieve, which can be helpful to leaders in their efforts to understand themselves and overcome those areas of their personalities that might threaten their effectiveness as leaders.

Defining the Battle

Even when these basic assumptions are acknowledged to some degree, many in the Christian community relegate the problem entirely to the realm of spiritual warfare and demonic attack. Fallen spiritual leaders are most often considered casualties in a cosmic spiritual battle and little else. But the problem is not that easily dismissed. With the emergence of the baby boom generation, and its members' ascendance to positions of leadership during the late 1970s and 1980s, America and the church discovered a generation plagued by a plethora of personal dysfunctions.[1] Whether it was the dysfunction of co-dependence, addictive behaviors, obsessive-compulsive disorder, narcissistic personality disorder, adult children of alcoholics (ACOA), or any one of a host of others, personal dysfunctions became the badge of the boomer generation and a focal point of church ministries.

As the boomers ascended to their leadership roles, they carried with them their various dysfunctions. The majority of tragically fallen Christian leaders during the past ten to fifteen years have been baby boomers who felt driven to achieve and succeed in an increasingly competitive and demanding church environment. Most often their ambition has been a subtle and dangerous combination of their own dysfunctional personal needs and a certain measure of altruistic desire to expand the kingdom of God. However, because ambition is easily disguised in Christian circles and couched in spiritual language (the need to fulfill the Great Commission and expand the church), the

15

dysfunctions that drive Christian leaders often go undetected and unchallenged until it is too late.

The Goals of the Book

While we can't promise to have all the answers, this book will help you accomplish three things. First, it will guide you in understanding what the dark side is. Second, it will assist you in identifying your own dark side. And third, it will give you some specific steps for overcoming the dark side lurking in your success before you get blindsided by it.

To address these three issues we have divided the book into three parts. In Part 1: Understanding Our Dark Side we will look closely at what the dark side is, how it develops, and the results it often creates. Then in Part 2: Discovering Our Dark Side we will review the five dark-side issues experienced most often by leaders and assist you in determining which one you are most likely to find in your own life. Finally in Part 3: Redeeming Our Dark Side we will offer a five-step plan for overcoming the dark side.

Before we can effectively begin to overcome our dark side and mitigate its negative effects, we must be able to identify the particular issues we struggle with and learn how they have become dark-side issues for us. This will require special understanding and insight, found in chapters 3 through 12. So resist the temptation to jump straight into the practical steps of part 3.

As we write this book, our prayer is that *Overcoming the Dark Side of Leadership* will be the first step on a lifelong journey of self-discovery for you, a journey that will lead you to a more fulfilling and effective life and ministry on behalf of our Lord and Savior, who promised us an abundant life.

ACKNOWLEDGMENTS

I f *Overcoming the Dark Side of Leadership* proves helpful to leaders at all, we owe much to those who have made its completion possible.

I (Sam) owe special thanks to my wife, Sue, who has taught me more about effective, balanced leadership than any book or class. Sue has kept me believing I could complete this project even when I had serious doubts. Her unconditional love, unwavering support, listening ear, and merciful heart have made me a better leader.

Sharon Reichwein, the office administrator at Eagle Heights Church, devoted countless and tireless hours to formatting, editing, and improving our manuscript. Without her highly professional efforts, this book would not have been completed with the same level of excellence it now bears. Words cannot fully convey our gratitude for her sacrificial service and personal friendship.

Dr. Sid Rogers has also been invaluable in the preparation of this manuscript. Sid has fielded numerous questions regarding writing style, content, and mechanics. Sid is a Christian leader who incarnates the principles of overcoming the dark side presented in part 3 of this book. His life and model have impacted us eternally.

I want to thank my coauthor, Gary L. McIntosh, for his continual encouragement—both in letters and conversation—to pursue this project. He is a professor who truly cares about his students and has been available to me not only as a doctoral student, but also as a pastor and now as a coauthor. His willingness to work with me on this manuscript has proven very helpful.

Together Gary and I thank our editors Paul Engle and Mary Suggs of Baker Publishing Group for their excellent work on this book. Their work has immensely enhanced its readability and quality. In addition several colleagues have graciously reviewed our manuscript and offered helpful suggestions for its improvement. While we cannot name them all, we thank them for their time and energy in this work.

Most of all, we are grateful to God for his grace and the privilege of being counted among the chosen and redeemed. Ultimately, if this work generates anything positive, the glory and praise must go to him.

INTRODUCTION
TO THE REVISED EDITION

In this new edition of *Overcoming the Dark Side of Leadership*, I (Sam) reflect on what I have experienced regarding leadership failures in the past ten years. I have included some new chapters and new insights throughout the text, as well as a more thorough and updated dark side profile in Appendix E.

In the preface to the first edition I wrote, "The majority of tragically fallen Christian leaders during the past ten to fifteen years have been baby boomers who felt driven to achieve and succeed in an increasingly competitive and demanding church environment" (p. 15). During the ten years since I wrote those words, I have had time to reflect and think even more deeply about leadership failures and their causes, particularly in the context of Christian leadership. And I have become more convinced than ever that the above quote reflects more truth than many of us would care to admit.

At the core of the problem is personal ambition and the insidious desire to have or possess something that is not able to be possessed—namely, success. We live in a culture obsessed with both *having* and *success*. And this desire has infiltrated the ranks of Christian leaders as it has every other strata of American culture. The problem arises from the fact that success is not something one can have or possess. True success is a state of *being* not *having*.

Unfortunately, many Christian leaders are driven manically to *have* success. In the church, having success is measured by how many people you have attending your service, the size of the facility you have, the number of staff members you have, how many user-friendly programs you have, and the size of the budget you have. As a result, leaders who need to have success to validate themselves are driven to acquire these things and are willing to pay virtually any price to do so. I have become convinced that the desire to have these things is not compatible with biblical concepts of church or even Christianity. As a result, even when these leaders succeed in creating a large congregation, a large facility, and all the other markers that measure success in the twenty-first-century church, they are no closer to actually *having* or *possessing* the inner feelings of success that they have been seeking through their manic activity. It is at this point that leaders often begin looking elsewhere in an effort to assuage their needs for personal validation and worth—needs they thought would be met by *having* a measure of success.

Moreover, this phenomenon is very often fueled by church leaders who are just as desperate to *have* success as the pastors and staff they seek to employ. Take for example this recent employment ad in *Leadership Journal*, placed by a church in New Jersey:

> ### IF YOU BUILD IT, HE (OR SHE) WILL COME
>
> We are looking for a Head of Staff who wants to build something big. We're a Christ-centered congregation in Summit, New Jersey. We believe that God has called us to do great things. And so we want to build something big too. Are you one of the great heads of staff out there? Think about the opportunity we have here. It is going to be exciting![1]

20

Imagine the person who responds to such an ad. They must consider themselves as one of the "great heads of staff" and be driven to "build something big." I don't believe a better recipe for church or leadership failure could be written!

But sadly, as I mentioned in the preface, because ambition is easily disguised in Christian circles and couched in spiritual language (the need to fulfill the Great Commission and expand the church), the dysfunctions that drive Christian leaders often go undetected and unchallenged until it is too late. And so the church begins mopping up yet another messy and often public leadership failure.

I am convinced that reducing the potential for leadership failures must begin with challenging the current paradigm of measuring success in terms of *having* as opposed to *being*. Unfortunately, "the alternative of *having* versus *being* does not appeal to common sense,"[2] as Erich Fromm wrote in his classic work *To Have or to Be?*

> *To have*, so it would seem, is a normal function of our life: in order to live we must have things. Moreover, we must have things in order to enjoy them. In a culture in which the supreme goal is to have—and to have more and more—and in which one can speak of someone as "being worth a million dollars," how can there be an alternative between having and being? On the contrary, it would seem that the very essence of being is having; that if one *has* nothing, one *is* nothing.[3]

Fromm articulates, I believe, the exact feelings of many contemporary pastors and church leaders who came of age in the last twenty years of the twentieth century. If they *have* nothing, they *are* nothing. *Being* has become inextricably linked to *having*.

Yet this is entirely contrary to all that Scripture teaches. Jesus said to his disciples, "Truly I tell you, unless you change and become like children, you will never enter the kingdom of heaven. Whoever becomes humble like this child is the greatest in the kingdom of heaven" (Matt. 18:3–4 NRSV). On another occasion Jesus told his disciples, "The greatest among you will *be* your servant. All who exalt themselves will be humbled, and all who humble themselves will *be* exalted" (Matt. 23:11–12 NRSV, emphasis mine). Jesus clearly saw kingdom success in terms of *being*, not in terms of *having* or even *doing*. Kingdom success is entirely counterintuitive and countercultural to those of us living in a consumer-oriented culture, which is hell-bent on possessing more and more stuff in an effort to *be* somebody.

The apostle Paul seems to have transitioned during his life journey from measuring his worth in terms of *having* to *being* when he wrote,

> Yet whatever gains I *had*, these I have come to regard as loss because of Christ. More than that, I regard everything as loss because of the surpassing value of *knowing* Christ Jesus my Lord. For his sake I have suffered the loss of all things, and I regard them as rubbish, in order that I may gain Christ and be found in him, not *having* a righteousness of my own that comes from the law, but one that comes through faith in Christ, the righteousness from God based on faith. I want to know Christ and the power of his resurrection and the sharing of his sufferings by *becoming* like him in his death.
>
> Philippians 3:7–10 NRSV, emphasis mine

Similarly, Erich Fromm wrote, "By *being* I refer to the mode of existence in which one neither *has* anything nor *craves to have* something, but is joyous, employs one's faculties productively, is *oned* to the world."[4] This is very much like what Paul writes when he states, "Not that I am referring to being in need; for I have learned to *be* content with whatever I have" (Phil. 4:11 NRSV, emphasis mine).

I firmly believe that if we could help pastors and Christian leaders make this paradigm shift in the way they view success and help them understand that the ultimate objective of the Christian faith is striving to *be* rather than striving to *have* or to *do*, we would greatly reduce the number of leadership failures within Christendom.

Encouragingly, since the initial publication of this book ten years ago, many seminaries and graduate schools have now begun to acknowledge the vital role of the leader's inner life—his or her state of being—in the exercise of public leadership. In most business schools, courses on ethics and the morality of leadership have been added to augment the traditional topics of marketing, finance, and management.

Many of the seminaries and theological schools responsible for preparing men and women for roles as clergy and leaders of nonprofit organizations in America have added a curricular focus on intentional character development. My own institution, Bethel Seminary, has completely reorganized itself around three centers, one of which is the Center for Spiritual and Personal Formation. These changes have been made in an effort to recognize the vital importance of *being* as opposed to merely *doing* or *having* when it comes to the exercise of effective kingdom leadership.

Though our institutions have done well to begin addressing these matters of personal character formation and the inner-life issues that all leaders must navigate on their leadership journey, ultimately it is the individual leader's responsibility to take full advantage of these opportunities and resources.

There comes a point in all leaders' lives—if they remain in leadership long enough—when they will begin to experience the relational friction, organizational blow-ups, and personal pain that result from unidentified and unresolved inner-life issues. When that time comes, they have a profound and pivotal choice to make: Will they allow that pain and chaos to serve as a catalyst that can take them deep into the recesses of their dark side and, as Annie Dillard has written, "ride the monster all the way down," allowing God to do his healing, restorative work in long-buried areas of personal pain and shame? Or will they put up their protective shield and refuse to take the journey? That critical decision will determine the future trajectory of not only their leadership but also their lives.

Unfortunately, there have been far too many leaders who have chosen to continue their attempts at personal-image management in the face of a dark side that is glaringly obvious to everyone but them, all in a pathetic attempt to save face and maintain their shining public persona rather than take the inward journey that leads to personal wholeness and holiness. But almost always in those cases, the dark side eventually brings down the curtain on those leaders in a dramatic and often destructive way. When we are faced with this choice in our life and leadership, we would do well to remember Carl Jung's warning: "The brighter the persona, the darker the shadow."[5]

My personal prayer and passion is that this revised edition of *Overcoming the Dark Side of Leadership* will be used by God to awaken many leaders to the dangers of the dark side and motivate them to finally take the most important journey of their life—the journey inward, accompanied by him who is the source of both light and life.

Samuel D. Rima

PART 1

UNDERSTANDING
OUR DARK SIDE

1

BLINDSIDED
BY THE
DARK SIDE

Like water exploding from behind a broken dam the words gushed out, laced with a frightening combination of anger and bitterness, "I quit! I just can't do this anymore! No matter what I do or how hard I work it's never the right thing and it's never good enough. I just can't please everyone! What do people expect from me anyway?"

It was my wife who became the unsuspecting and unfortunate victim of this tidal wave of emotion. We were driving to visit some friends when my emotional dam burst, catching my wife completely by surprise. Without warning, my previously well-ordered inner world reeled out of control. The tears gushed uncontrollably, and I felt completely lost. I simply could not think clearly or regain my inner balance. It was as if a huge, ominous, dark cloud covered me, and for the first time in my life I had no hope. So sudden and overwhelming was the emotional onslaught, I felt the only solution was to quit the ministry.

What was it that had sparked such a powerful outburst in the middle of what was by all definitions a very successful and effective season of ministry? Had it come during a time of professional frustration or failure, it might have been easily explained and understood. But coming as it did after two years of tremendous ministry growth, the completion of a relocation into our church's first facility, and a very satisfying home life, it was confusing and frightening. What was happening to me? Why did I feel like I was having a breakdown? Where did this anger, depression, and feeling of abject failure come from so suddenly? Why did it occur at this time, in this way, and at this place?

The answer may surprise you. I had been blindsided by the dark side.

What Is the Dark Side?

The dark side, though sounding quite sinister, is actually a natural result of human development. It is the inner urges, compulsions, and dysfunctions of our personality that often go unexamined or remain unknown to us until we experience an emotional explosion, as just described in Sam's life, or some other significant problem that causes us to search for a reason why.[1] Because it is a part of us that we are unaware of to some degree, lurking in the shadows of our personality, we have labeled it the dark side of our personality. However, in spite of the foreboding mental image the term *dark side* creates, it is not, as we shall see, exclusively a negative force in our lives. In almost every case the factors that eventually undermine us are shadows of the ones that contribute to our success.

At times the dark side seems to leap on us unexpectedly. In reality it has slowly crept up on us. The development of our dark side has been a lifetime in the making despite the fact that the assault by these powerful emotions, compulsions, and dysfunctions can be sudden. Like vinegar and soda being slowly swirled together in a tightly closed container, our personalities have been slowly intermingled with examples, emotions, expectations, and experiences that over a lifetime have created our dark side.

If not tended, the mixture will ultimately explode with great ferocity. For some, the lid can be kept on for quite a period of time before the explosion finally occurs. Others sense the strange stirrings and ominous bubbling deep inside, and not knowing for certain what is taking place, they periodically release a little of the pressure by lifting the lid in a solitary act of frustration or some other form of emotional release. Yet for others, those foreign stirrings deep within are denied, ignored, explained away, and even completely repressed until finally the container can expand no more and it explodes in a sudden and massive moral failure or some other unexpected, shocking, or bizarre behavior. This denial and repression along with the resulting emotional explosion are particularly common among religious leaders who feel the constant need to be in total control of their lives so they can minister effectively to others. Regardless of how sudden the explosion may seem, it has been in the making since childhood.

Sam's Story

I (Sam) grew up in a healthy, loving Christian home. There was no abuse—not emotional, not verbal, not physical. In fact I had parents whose primary priority in life was the well-being and development of their children. This is not a literary catharsis in which my parents are blamed for the issues I must deal with as an adult. My parents were not perfect but they did their best, and I was aware of that even as a child. However, the way I interpreted and synthesized the examples I saw and the lessons they taught was not always balanced and correct.

My father has been the single most influential person in my life. I have never known or been aware of another person with such drive and determination, coupled with an unrivaled work ethic. I remember him holding down two and three different jobs at a time in an effort to provide for our family. He also found the time and energy to remodel our house, coach our baseball teams, and help out in our Boy Scout troops. Growing up I can never remember hearing my father complain. Now I am sure he must have complained at times, but never enough to leave a lasting impression on a watching and listening little boy. As I worked with my father raking leaves in the yard and doing projects around the house, the one thing I clearly learned was that if a job was worth doing at all, it was worth doing as perfectly as you were able. We were never allowed to settle for second best when it came to doing a job. If you did the job to just get by, you would eventually pay for it. That is the way my father has worked and lived.

As positive as this example was, the way I integrated it into my life provided the seeds of my dark side. I found myself even as a youngster needing the approval of others—especially my father. It was not enough merely to finish a job and do it well; I needed to be assured by Dad that the job was up to par and in fact had exceeded his expectations. Anything less was failure.

My religious upbringing provided fertile soil for the growth of my dark side. The Pentecostal church I grew up in was one in which a subtle legalism ruled the lives of its people. Because one's relationship with God was based to a great extent on behavior, you were never quite sure where you stood spiritually after a week of being soiled by the sinful world. This lack of spiritual assurance led to repeated rededications each Sunday evening. It seemed that keeping God happy was a difficult and nearly impossible job—but it had to be done.

However, if you were able to keep God happy and he was pleased with the purity and sincerity of your life, you would be blessed with the baptism in the Spirit, as evidenced by speaking in other tongues. It was God's ultimate stamp of approval for a job well done. Unfortunately, after several years of youth camp "Holy Spirit Nights," countless rallies, and untold numbers of revival meetings, I never received the much coveted blessing. It was clear to me as a sixteen-year-old boy that I was not pleasing to God or I most certainly would have received his gift. I reasoned that I simply needed to work harder for it. However, God's approval never came. I was sorely disappointed and destined to live out my days with second-best spirituality—something I had learned I should never accept. But my attempts to gain God's smile of favor didn't cease. I simply began working harder. Like raking fall leaves in the backyard of my childhood home to impress my father, maybe I could impress God and gain his approval by working hard.

I continued my pursuit of God's approval in seminary. Maybe if I gave my life in service to God it would result in his long-awaited blessing. Seminary proved to be an environment in which I thrived. Not only did it provide an atmosphere that demanded hard work, but also it provided the immediate feedback I had craved for so long. Because there was an objective standard to judge the quality of my performance (grades and the comments of professors) and because this was spiritual activity, it seemed as if each grade was being given by the hand of God himself. During my seminary years the craving for God's approval seemed temporarily satisfied, but that satisfaction was short-lived. I was still a person in search of approval. It was a search I could not completely understand or describe. I did know that no matter how much approval I received, it never seemed to satisfy the craving that ate away deep inside.

I began my collision course with the dark side the day I entered pastoral ministry in a local church. In church ministry the objective standard for judging my performance, and thus God's approval, was missing.

My first assignment as a senior pastor was with a newly forming congregation in a rapidly developing community of Southern California. The small group of excited believers had no building of their own, no office facility for a pastor, and not even the financial resources to pay a salary without denominational assistance. It was a tailor-made situation for a person eager to please and see tangible signs of success.

The first year of that ministry we saw much success. Unfortunately our standard of success had been reduced to numeric growth and economic expansion. As long as I could keep the ministry expanding in ways that my board and denominational superiors could see, I felt a measure of approval. But there was always more to be done, always more leaves to be raked, and others in the tree just waiting to fall as soon as those were raked up.

Verbal approval from parishioners and board members slowed to a trickle, eventually drying up altogether as success and growth became expected. When it was slow the questions of why came with devastating impact. I thought I simply needed to work harder to maintain the successes that would result in the words of approval that had begun to drive my life and motivate every decision. But there comes a time when you can't rake any faster and the leaves just keep falling. An entry from my personal journal records the day I realized I couldn't work hard enough to meet the expectations I felt constantly pressing in on me:

> For the last two and a half years I have worked hard (but never hard enough). I have counseled (but never with enough compassion). We have socialized and shared (but never with enough people). Sure, the church has grown, but not fast enough or well enough according to my internal standard. In many ways I haven't come to terms with how the church has grown and won't even allow myself to believe that it has. It's as if I'm always waiting for the other shoe to drop and the whole thing will fall apart. As a result, I work even harder to hold things together and keep them from falling apart. (15 September 1990)

Two days after my outburst in the car with my wife, I penned those words in a Florida hotel room as I took my first tenuous steps in the lifelong process of exploring my dark side. I slowly began to realize that paradoxically the personality traits and inner drives that brought me success as a leader were also what had ultimately caused my desperation. I began to wonder if I were an aberration or some sort of spiritually and emotionally defective leader. Had anyone else ever felt the cold shadow of the dark side as I had?

32

We Never Walk Alone

Since that frightening, life-changing encounter with his dark side, Sam has learned that his was not and is not a unique experience. It is a paradox that all leaders face sooner or later. The aspects of life that push us in a positive way toward success can also exert a negative pull, destroying our effectiveness. As a leader you have no doubt experienced this paradox yourself.

It does not matter in what arena you lead others. You may be a CEO of a large multimillion-dollar corporation or the sole proprietor of a smaller home-based company. Perhaps you work as a middle manager or pastor a church. Maybe you are president of your school's parent-teacher association or a fraternal organization or you teach junior high school. Wherever and in whatever capacity you lead others, you need to understand your own dark side.

I (Gary) discovered years ago that we need to understand our dark side even as parents and spouses. Like most pastors I was always expected to have the answers to emotional, theological, and administrative questions at church. Later, when I began consulting with churches, I again found myself in a situation where those I counseled depended on me for the correct answer. In one form or another, my entire professional life has been devoted to telling others the answers to their questions and needs. Unfortunately this ability to diagnose a situation and prescribe a solution, which brought me success in professional life, turned out to have a dark side when expressed in family relationships.

A person who must always have the answer usually does not listen very well. I fell into the trap of always giving answers to my wife and children when all they wanted was for me to listen. The talents and abilities that made me successful in work had a corresponding dark side that made me less effective at home.

After seeking help with a Christian counselor, I discovered several other aspects of my dark side that were undermining my effectiveness as a leader. Anger and hurt from being abandoned by my father when I was a child were driving me to succeed as a way of winning his favor. Harmful communication patterns, which had existed for several generations on my mother's side of the family, were being duplicated in my own life. If these destructive tendencies had not been recognized, admitted, and addressed, I may have lost my family in the process of winning the world.

Sam's explosion described earlier resulted in a two-week trip to Florida (at the recommendation of his church board) so that he could sort through the emotional debris left in the wake of his encounter with the dark side. Gary's discovery led to a year of counseling, where he faced his dark side and began slowly to redeem it. Both of us are fortunate. We survived, but not all encounters with the dark side end so benignly. As we will discover in future chapters, leaders often suffer significant failures when they do not understand and control their dark side.

TARGETING INSIGHTS

- The "dark side" refers to our inner urges, compulsions, motivations, and dysfunctions that drive us toward success or undermine our accomplishments.
- Our dark side develops slowly over a lifetime of experiences and is often revealed in moments of frustration or anger.
- The dark side is a normal development of life and can be an agent for both good and bad in our lives.

APPLYING INSIGHTS

Reflect on Sam's story and how his dark side collided with his life work.

In what ways have you experienced similar collisions in your own life,

work, family, or leadership role?

2

DANGER
ON THE
DARK SIDE

In his powerful and insightful book *Let Your Life Speak*, Parker Palmer writes that we as leaders have the power to cast either shadow or light by the exercise of our leadership. Palmer further contends that we as leaders create the ethos in which others must live: one of light in which people flourish and grow, or one as shadowy as hell that will bring pain and death.

Why is it that we always assume that our leadership is good? Why do we believe that our vision for God's church is always the right vision and that for anyone to question or challenge our vision is tantamount to insubordination against God himself? The sad reality is that all too often, when we are living and leading from the shadow of our dark side, danger lurks around virtually every corner, not only for us but also for the people and organizations that we lead.

Driven to Danger

After serving as senior pastor for fifteen years in a medium-sized urban church on the east coast, Tim was more than eager to entertain the advances of a call committee from a larger church in Southern California. Tim had been recommended to the chairman of the call committee by one of his seminary classmates who thought he knew Tim relatively well.

As Tim and the call committee successfully navigated the usual rituals required of a pastoral search process, Tim began to feel a vague sense of uneasiness. Though this was the opportunity for which he'd been waiting ever since leaving seminary, he worried about whether or not he was up to the task of leading a larger, multiple-staff church. But rather than acknowledge his concerns and share them with his wife, Carol, or the chair of the call committee, Tim convinced himself that his uneasiness was unfounded and decided instead to project an air of absolute confidence in his ability to provide leadership for this new church, which was more than triple the size of the previous congregation he had served.

During the final stages of the search process, Tim answered questions about how he would manage the staff of fifteen with great detail and assurances that he and the staff would work together like a well-oiled machine. He handled congregational inquires into how he would oversee the $5 million budget and increasingly challenging space problems with creativity and aplomb. Despite his nagging doubts and concerns, even Tim was beginning to believe this new leadership challenge would be a piece of cake. After all, he'd convinced himself, half the battle was making others believe he knew how to lead at this advanced level, even though he was riddled with self-doubt and feelings of insecurity. Tim believed that expressing his concerns and being transparent about his feelings would only foster a lack of confidence in his leadership. After all, Tim reasoned, he'd made it this far, hadn't he?

So, rather than approach the new position with a sense of healthy humility and communicate that he was willing to learn from the more experienced staff members and truly work as a team in this new leadership venture, Tim had settled on the approach of "never let them see you sweat."

Ultimately, Tim was called to the church with a strong congregational vote and immediately set out to make his mark. Three years into his new ministry position, Tim found himself in an extremely challenging position as senior pastor. Based on the leadership books he'd been reading, he decided to hire an executive pastor to essentially run the church. This person would be the primary interface with and supervisor of all the staff, allowing Tim to insulate himself from hands-on management of the staff. He would devote himself to preaching and writing and delegate congregational care matters to the pastor of congregational care.

To address the space challenges the church faced, Tim launched a compelling effort to convince the leadership and congregation that what the church needed was an entirely new sanctuary, preschool, and office/classroom complex. Not only would this massive building project meet their current facility needs, it would also serve to attract new members to the church, who would then be able to help pay for the $15 million project.

Tim would not allow anything to defeat his dream of building an even larger facility that he hoped would allow him to become the pastor of a true megachurch, although there had been significant pockets of congregational resistance to the building plans and the ensuing capital campaign. Many of those uncomfortable with the plans felt that the current membership would not be able to service the $7 million debt the church would have to take on.

Among the resisters was a popular staff member who had been on staff for the past ten years. As the pastor of children's ministries, Stacy had a significant following that was composed of the parents and grandparents of the many children she had helped during the previous decade. Though Stacy was willing to move ahead with the church, she made it known that she was not in favor of the building project and felt that the debt would cripple the church's ministry as they pinched every penny. Though Stacy had committed not to share her views publicly or to undermine the project in any way, Tim felt that her failure to fully support the project was a direct repudiation of his vision and leadership as the senior pastor. Stacy's refusal to embrace the building program reinforced Tim's secret feelings of insecurity as well as his personal doubts about exercising leadership in a significantly larger church. Moreover, Tim interpreted Stacy's lack of support for the building program as a lack of personal support for him as both a person and a leader. Thus, Stacy's position was not something Tim could allow himself to live with. He required total, enthusiastic support from every staff person. Anything less was seen as a challenge to him personally.

Ultimately, Pastor Tim felt that Stacy needed to either fully embrace the building program—and thus his leadership—or resign her position. Tim believed that to allow her to remain on staff was a threat to the staff team. However, rather than personally deal with Stacy regarding the issue and negotiate an appropriate solution to the situation, Tim met with his inner circle of elders and the executive pastor to plot out a strategy to remove Stacy from her position. During the following year, as the building program was in progress, Tim and his inner circle began to look for any signs of insubordination or poor performance that they could use to legitimize their removal of Pastor Stacy.

After nearly a year of trying to build a case against Stacy, Tim felt the time had finally arrived to play his hand and force Stacy from her position at the church. Tim decided that the best way to handle her removal would be through the executive pastor, Andrew, Stacy's direct supervisor.

The letter that informed her she was being removed for poor performance came as a complete shock to Stacy. Her most recent performance reviews, performed by Andrew, had been exemplary, so the list of petty complaints cited in the letter left Stacy confused and angry. She was told that failure to voluntarily resign, therefore acknowledging the legitimacy of the charges, would be grounds for immediate dismissal.

As word of the effort to remove Stacy was leaked to members of the congregation (not by Stacy), many people began to express their own anger and pent-up frustration with the direction in which the church had been moving since Tim had become senior pastor. Because Stacy refused to sign the letter and acknowledge the legitimacy of the charges, the board sent out a letter informing the congregation of a meeting at which Stacy's removal for poor performance would be voted on.

The congregational letter, however, resulted in a massive backlash that began to focus attention on Tim's leadership style, which appeared to many to be dictatorial, rigid, and highly impersonal. Rather than people supporting the removal of Pastor Stacy, people wondered how the situation with Stacy could have gotten so bad without them having been informed of it earlier. The meeting that had been called to discuss and vote on Stacy's removal instead turned into a referendum on Tim's leadership. The congregation's response to the situation was an even greater threat to Tim's feelings of insecurity and lack of confidence. With the new buildings scheduled to open later that year, Tim found himself struggling with severe depression, contemplating resignation from the church, and wondering whether he was even fit for pastoral ministry.

When Our Dark Side Endangers Others

Pastor Tim isn't the only leader who has experienced the pain that can result when a personal dysfunction such as acute insecurity is ignored and covered over with a mask of confidence. In fact, leaders that we perceive to be exceptionally confident and in command are often compensating for a deeply rooted sense of inferiority and insecurity. We see this dynamic operating in the lives of comedians, actors, and models. Some of the most beautiful models in the world express personal feelings of insecurity regarding their appearance. Some of the funniest comedians admit that their larger-than-life public persona is an attempt to compensate for deeply rooted feelings of inferiority and to deal with the pain that resulted from childhood teasing and trauma. And the same can be true for those who aspire to positions of leadership, whether it is in the political, business, or religious realm.

When we refuse to process in healthy ways feelings of insecurity, unhealthy codependence issues, feelings of personal shame, deeply sublimated anger or fear, or some combination of these or other issues, they will wreak havoc in our lives and leadership and eventually endanger ourselves and others.

NASA mission specialist Lisa Nowak had achieved what few men, let alone women, have been able to accomplish: she had become an astronaut and flew a mission on the space shuttle. Those who knew her admired and respected her as an effective leader, a loving mother, and an extremely brilliant woman. She had been the valedictorian of her high school, earned a master's degree in aeronautical engineering from the United States Naval Academy, learned to fly fighter jets, and risen to the rank of captain in the navy. Friends described Lisa as funny and a nice person to be with.

But in February 2007, Lisa Nowak got into her car—which was loaded with a knife, latex gloves, a raft of emails between two fellow astronauts, and a BB gun—and drove nine hundred miles from Houston to Orlando, wearing an adult diaper, allegedly to assault a woman she perceived was trying to steal her love interest.[1]

Upon word of her arrest and the charge of attempted murder, her parents reacted with shocked disbelief and told interviewers, "Considering both her personal and professional life, these alleged events are completely out of character and have come as a tremendous shock to our family."[2] Evidently there was another side to Lisa's shining public persona: a darker side of which others, even her family, were unaware. But, as Jung said, "The brighter the persona, the darker the shadow."

At the time of this writing, Lisa awaits trial on attempted murder charges, and her public explosion has left her children without their mother, her family hurt and confused, and NASA with yet another blotch on its already spotty reputation.

But as we know, it's not just pastors and astronauts who have had to experience the danger of the dark side as a result of neglecting it. In the ten years since this book was originally published, our country has been rocked by a series of high-profile leadership failures that have endangered the lives and livelihoods of many innocent people.

Dangerous Success

Sammy Waksal was the son of immigrants. His parents, Ellie and Abram Waksal, were the only members of their extended families to survive the concentration camps of Hitler's Third Reich. After their liberation by Allied troops, they serendipitously met for the first time and married shortly after the war's end. They began a family, and taking whatever work they could find to put food on the table, they attempted to find stable jobs that would provide security and the possibility of prosperity, which would help their children advance beyond the family's current economic and social station.

However, with the continent still covered in post-war rubble and the prospects for a successful future in short supply, the newlyweds decided to flee Europe in search of a better life, a life where their success would result from their willingness to work. After much consideration, Ellie and Abram set their sights on the United States with hopes of securing for themselves and their family a share in the American Dream.

Growing up in the home of concentration camp survivors intent on exchanging their Nazi-style suffering for American-style success, Sammy learned at an early age that success was available to those willing to work for it. He also began to learn what success looked like. Success had to do with money and the things money could buy. If he ever hoped to be successful and help fulfill his parents' dream for the family, he knew doing so would involve making enough money so he could live in the right community, afford a house befitting a successful American, drive the kind of car that accompanied such a house, and enjoy a lifestyle that clearly broadcast his success for all to see.

With this dream of success firmly planted in his mind, Sammy began his quest. He worked hard to do well in school, realizing that a good education would be essential to his quest. As a result, Sammy, now known by the more mature moniker "Sam," began his undergraduate education in Florida before transferring to Ohio State University, where he excelled academically. He then advanced to pursue a PhD in microbiology and immunology at Princeton University (ultimately receiving his degree from Ohio State University). Sam was on his way to finding the success he longed for—the success he knew would erase the memories of growing up in a modest house and the stigma he felt by belonging to a family of Jewish immigrants.

As Dr. Samuel K. Waksal, Sam enjoyed the admiration and respect that seemed inherent in the letters "PhD." With a sterling academic record and reputation, the newly minted Dr. Waksal secured a highly-competed-for and prestigious research fellowship at Stanford University, an absolute dream job for any new graduate. But for Sam, the drive for success would never allow him to feel comfortable in any one place for too long. Lack of movement, in his driven mind, was equated with mediocrity and stalling on the quest. It was always onward and upward until he finally arrived at a level of success that would once and for all assuage his secret feelings of inferiority and his desperate thirst for a truly significant life.

His quest led him from one prestigious position to another, each one connecting him with key people across the country and providing critical experiences he knew he could leverage into still bigger and better opportunities for success and significance.

Along the way, though, Sam began to recognize that each new, more prestigious position didn't seem to provide the sense of inner fulfillment and significance he had at one time felt sure it would. Instead, with each of these advancements he was left with an inner emptiness that served only to spur him on in his search for the perfect position that would be his personal Valhalla. There was something taking place in the deep recesses of his life that seemed to prevent him from experiencing the success he was seeking.

Eventually, as a result of his many connections and contacts, Sam came across an opportunity with the potential to deliver a degree of success that few people ever realize. He was turned on to a new antibody protocol that was being developed to treat colorectal cancer, one of the leading forms of cancer, by specifically targeting the cancer cells and blocking their ability to feed themselves, thus starving them to death. The antibody was in its early stages of development and experimentation, but early tests produced remarkable results and presented almost unbelievable potential for the antibody as a new cancer treatment. Because of a relationship with the Stanford scientist who had discovered the new antibody, Sam was given the opportunity to license and further develop this potentially life-saving treatment. It was an opportunity full of risk, but in Sam's mind the potential for vast rewards far outweighed the risks. It was also a decision that would finally give him the opportunity to launch and lead his own company.

If Sam were able to bring this experimental treatment to market as a new cancer drug, it promised to make him and anyone else on the ground floor of his company more money than they had ever thought possible. Sam knew this was his shot to realize his quest for success and finally experience the sense of inner fulfillment and significance he had longed for his entire life. This was his chance to validate his parents' sacrifices and hard work and make them truly proud.

In 1984 Sam and his three partners selected the name ImClone for their new company and set in motion the long process of bringing Erbitux, their miracle cancer drug, to market. Along the way, they decided to take the company public in an effort to raise the necessary capital and keep the company's groundbreaking work moving forward. They issued an IPO in 1991, and Sam Waksal became a multimillionaire overnight.

After years of dreaming and working and striving for the upper echelons of society—that place where Sam knew success would at last be his—he arrived. He now had more money than any one person really needed and could buy virtually anything he desired. For Sam Waksal, the dream house was no longer just a dream. He could drive any car he desired and park it in the most affluent community he could find. Everything he'd ever dreamed of was his—all of those things he believed would bring him success and the accompanying sense of fulfillment, purpose, and personal worth. Sam owned a multimillion-dollar apartment in Manhattan, a luxurious estate in the Hamptons, millions of dollars' worth of original art, beautiful boats, and exotic cars. He socialized with the rich and famous as he jet-setted around the globe.

But ultimately, none of it was enough to satisfy the yearning deep in Sam's soul. The stark reality that he had finally clawed his way to the top and achieved the American Dream but still felt empty inside—possibly even more empty than when he had first set out on his quest—left him depressed and confused. What more could he possibly need to achieve or acquire in order to feel successful and feel that his life had purpose?

In his desperate quest to find success that truly mattered, Sam began to borrow huge sums of money, securing the loans with the value of his ImClone stock portfolio, so that he could buy even more things and upgrade his already lavish lifestyle. At one point, even with his stock holdings worth hundreds of millions of dollars, Sam carried a personal debt of more than

$188 million. If the Food and Drug Administration approved Erbitux, as everyone expected, the debt would be no problem at all. But if for some unexpected reason the approval were denied, it would be catastrophic for Sam Waksal.

Just after Christmas in 2001, while vacationing in the Caribbean, Sam received a phone call that threatened to bring his quest to a screeching halt. He learned that the FDA would be sending a letter to ImClone, stating that they had declined approval of Erbitux because of shoddy scientific trials. Once this news hit the media, ImClone's stock price would fall precipitously. It would be a financial bloodbath. Just as Sam had become wealthy overnight at the time of ImClone's IPO, he now faced the very real possibility of losing that wealth in the same way. If his ImClone stock crashed, his millions of dollars in loans would be quickly called in because he would no longer have the collateral to support the debt.

In an effort to stave off almost certain bankruptcy and public humiliation—a fear Sam had been working all of his life to overcome—he sold a huge amount of his personal ImClone holdings, based on his secret knowledge about the impending letter from the FDA. He called his father and some close friends, telling them to sell their ImClone holdings as well. To Sam, nothing would signify failure more than causing his elderly father, who had sacrificed and survived so much in life, to end his life in poverty and see his son publicly humiliated. Sam was willing to behave illegally in an effort to protect his hard-won public persona.

Today Sam Waksal is in a federal prison, serving a ten-year sentence for securities fraud, insider trading, and obstruction of justice. The day FBI agents led him away in handcuffs from his multimillion-dollar SoHo loft, his public humiliation was beamed around the world. The very thing he feared most in life and had worked so hard for many years to avoid had become the paradoxical fruit of his own dark side.[3]

Different Dark Side, Same Dangers

The ImClone debacle came close on the heels of the American economy and thousands of retirees being blindsided by the Enron corporate scandal. Enron's failure bankrupted thousands of Americans who had heavily invested in its stock, destroyed the historic Arthur Anderson accounting firm, and helped nudge the national economy into a tailspin. Though the details were different from those of the ImClone fiasco, the dark-side issues that spawned Enron's downfall were amazingly similar: leaders with deep, unarticulated yearnings for success, a need for personal validation, and a deep desire for a sense of worth became victims of their own dark side.

When leaders refuse to take that inward journey to explore and resolve the inner-life issues that spawn the feelings described above, the result is almost always an explosion that spews its deadly shrapnel into the lives of others.

In March 2007, New Life Church in Colorado Springs, Colorado, announced the layoff of just fewer than fifty employees as a result of a significant financial shortfall that was precipitated by the departure of its senior pastor, Ted Haggard. Pastor Haggard was forced to resign as a result of homosexual activity and drug use that he had kept precariously tucked away in the shadow side of his personality. He had felt the friction and bubbling of something in his inner life for many years, but he had never been entirely willing or completely able to deal with those issues, and ultimately they exploded in a disaster that has painfully impacted many people.

Time and space do not allow us to write about all the failures such as the pedophilia scandal in the Catholic Church that has scarred thousands of people and bankrupted entire dioceses; the number of female schoolteachers arrested and convicted for becoming sexually involved with their young male students; and the members of Congress, both from the House and the Senate, convicted of crimes ranging from ethical violations to sexual crimes. But if we did have the time or inclination to list

46

just the high-profile cases, it would begin to feel as if we were beating a dead horse.

Our intention is not to belabor these tragic leadership failures. Rather, we want to communicate the incredible danger that is possible when we allow ourselves and others to be victimized by the dark side because of our failure or refusal to take that inward journey and "ride the monster all the way down," regardless of the pain it may cause us. As you read the following chapters, bear in mind that the pain required to confront our dark side and begin the process of overcoming it will be directly proportionate to the danger, destruction, humiliation, and shame we will avoid.

Targeting Insights

- Leaders have the power to cast either shadow or light by the exercise of their leadership, thus creating the ethos in which others must live.
- Leaders' dark sides can cause them to make unwise, risky, and even bizarre decisions that have the potential to harm themselves and those they lead or serve.
- When leaders refuse to take the inward journey to explore and resolve their dark side issues, the result will often be some form of leadership failure.

Applying Insights

Take some time to honestly reflect on whether some of the friction, conflicts, or challenges you face in leadership might be related to your unresolved dark side issues. Are you willing to take action and begin dealing with your dark side issues? Why or why not?

3

COMPANY
ON THE
DARK SIDE

As a spiritual leader he had achieved amazing popularity. He had unequaled intellectual abilities and a morality that was absolute yet sensitized by the realities of daily life in such a way that it removed any appearance of self-righteousness. His communication skills were unrivaled by any of his local contemporaries. He preached with a passion, emotion, and eloquence that belied his young age and relative inexperience. In fact other pastors in his city, older and more experienced than he, envied his gift for public speaking and the obvious impact it had on his congregation and all others who were exposed to his teaching ministry. His congregation saw their young pastor as God's gift to them. Because of his willingness to be transparent in the pulpit and share his own shortcomings and struggles with sin, his parishioners actually could be heard calling him a "miracle of holiness." His ministry was having an incredible impact on the city of Boston.

But in spite of his God-given gifts and super-effective ministry, the young pastor had a secret life unknown to any of his church members. Even as he preached with power and emotion, his inner life was reeling dangerously out of control. The young pastor had committed adultery with a married woman in the church and she had become pregnant with his child. The congregation castigated the young woman as a promiscuous product of society but continued to hold their young minister in high esteem because the young woman refused to reveal the identity of the father of her child.

As agonizing as it was, the young leader had learned how to rationalize and hide his secret. But the more he rationalized or ignored his gross moral failure, the more tortured his life became. His dark secret caused him to become physically ill. As the emotional and physical burden continued to grow, the lid on his secret life began to bulge from the pressure of the volatile mixture within. The incongruity between his secret life and professional life eventually grew into a chasm he could no longer bridge with intellectual excuses. That vast gulf between his two worlds and the resulting emotional pressure he experienced eventually resulted in a breakdown, public humiliation, and an early death. This young, successful pastor's name was Rev. Arthur Dimmesdale, and he was the tortured Puritan pastor in Nathaniel Hawthorne's classic work *The Scarlet Letter*, set in seventeenth-century Boston.[1]

We need to realize that we are not alone in our struggle against the dark side and that it is not exclusive to twentieth-century televangelists and the pastors of today's megachurches. There is plenty of company on the dark side. In fact there have been Rev. Dimmesdales in every age and they abound today.

Victims Abound

At thirty-seven years of age, Lee (not his real name) was the senior pastor of the largest, fastest-growing church in the state.

In a relatively brief period of time, he had led this traditional, mainline church from an attendance of approximately five hundred worshipers to the point where their 1995 Easter service attracted fifty-five hundred worshipers, with major coverage on every local newscast and in the city's major newspaper. As a result of the dramatic growth under Lee's leadership, the church relocated from its modest five-hundred-seat sanctuary and thirty-thousand-square-foot facility to a three-hundred-thousand-square-foot former manufacturing plant on the interstate. Relocation to the new facility and subsequent renovation required an energetic leader, a thirteen-million-dollar price tag, and many years of work. But the church, leaders, and pastor seemed up to the task.

The church attracted many hurting people from dysfunctional backgrounds, and they found healing and a sense of belonging as they sat under the compassionate, relevant, and emotional messages delivered by their church's dynamic young pastor. Pastor Lee seemed to be able to relate to those struggling to live the life of faith in a way that few ministers could. His openness in the pulpit drew people by the thousands.

Lee seemed driven to achieve an extraordinary level of success. Every aspect of the church's ministry reflected Lee's emphasis on excellence and relevancy. The ministry he was building was amazing, the apparent work of God.

Tragically, on May 15, 1995, the bottom fell out of Lee's life and ministry. After a board meeting late that night, he drove to a local park and there, inexplicably, he exposed himself to a stranger and began masturbating in front of him. The stranger turned out to be an undercover police officer who was responding to numerous complaints about sexually illicit behavior allegedly taking place in the park. Pastor Lee was cited and charged with indecent exposure and lewd conduct.[2] He was devastated and tried to explain to the officer that his bizarre and shocking behavior resulted from an abusive past. On May 31, 1995, the same paper that had heralded his many amazing successes now announced his tragic and shocking fall.

Rather than acknowledge his offense and begin exploring the issues that might have precipitated it, he chose to construct an implausible excuse and he engaged a damage-control attorney. He was in denial.

Two consultants who had worked closely with this pastor in helping to facilitate the church's tremendous growth commented that his fall wasn't completely surprising to them. He seemed to have a dark side that was evident to others, at least in a minimal way, but was unacknowledged or at least unexamined by the pastor himself.

On August 2, 1995, Pastor Lee was found guilty of the charges against him and began an extended leave of absence from his expanding ministry, presumably as a precursor to his removal as pastor by his denomination.[3] Pastor Lee is a victim of the dark side but he is hardly alone.

From Visions of Grandeur to Grand Failure

On May 6, 1987, the Assemblies of God defrocked Jim Bakker, founder of the Praise the Lord (PTL) television ministry and Christian theme park Heritage U.S.A., for an adulterous encounter with Jessica Hahn and allegations of bisexual activity.[4] In addition to his denominational troubles, Bakker served seven years of a forty-five-year sentence in federal prison for wire fraud and conspiracy that involved bilking supporters out of millions of dollars. His moral failures brought untold disgrace and shame to the cause of Christ and further reinforced an already cynical public view of Christianity.

Prior to his conviction the troubled televangelist attempted to explain his problems:

> I should have been more attentive to more details, but I had a vision and a plan, and I was a man with a fire inside of me to do something for the Christian world. . . . And to see that dream gone, it hurts. It's been living death. It would have been kinder for these men to assassinate us than do what they've done to

us . . . we do things flamboyant . . . I dream, I dream. I have to work. And I dream of building another city, maybe in California. And I dream of going back on television someday.[5]

Even to the bitter end, Jim Bakker refused to admit or was totally unaware of how his personality and dysfunctions had contributed to the problems he faced. To him, it was simply a matter of being misunderstood.[6]

How could a man who accomplished such amazing organizational feats have so little perspective on himself and the magnitude of the chaos he had created? What could cause a person to be such an astounding success and at the same time such a dismal, shameful failure? He was blinded by the dark side of his personality, and his visions of grandeur ended in nothing but grand failure.

Not all encounters with the dark side are as scandalous and dramatic as Jim Bakker's PTL debacle or Pastor Lee's lewd conduct conviction. Not every foray on the dark side ends with such devastating consequences. But whenever the dark side is encountered it is a frightening and sobering experience.

Coming Apart at the Seams

Bill Hybels has not experienced significant public failure that would leave a lasting blemish on his leadership. He has been a leader of integrity. In fact he is one of the most admired, respected, and successful church leaders in America today, overseeing one of the largest, most innovative Protestant congregations in the United States. In spite of his success and leadership effectiveness, Bill Hybels has fought many painful skirmishes with the dark side of his personality, some of which have brought him to the verge of emotional breakdown.

Growing up in Kalamazoo, Michigan, Bill was expected to take his place alongside his father in the family's wholesale produce company. From an early age Bill learned the importance of doing a job well and staying at a task until it was completed, regardless of the demands it might make physically or emotionally.

> The clearest illustration of the work ethic passed from father to son was the day Bill had to empty a truckload of rotten potatoes. After hours of unloading bag after bag of slimy, smelly potatoes, he complained to his father about the number of bags still remaining. "Don't worry Billy," his father said, "you only have to unload them one bag at a time." . . . Over the years [Bill's] ability to face any challenge "one bag at a time" has served him well.[7]

Bill Hybels learned his childhood lessons well, maybe too well. No matter how daunting the task, he would not quit until the job was done, and done well. Unfortunately, when the task involves leading and managing a growing church of fourteen-thousand-plus, it is impossible to ever finish the task. The only solution? Work harder. Keep at it, one bag at a time, until the job is finally done. But as soon as he would remove one smelly bag of ministry potatoes, three more would take its place. His frantic psychological need to "unload the truck" led to a workaholic lifestyle that required virtually every minute of every day. It was this warped view of a work ethic inculcated during childhood that nearly led to a complete emotional breakdown.

> By December 1989 Bill was working seven days a week, coming home only to recuperate enough to get back to work. But he had reached his breaking point. One Saturday, just a few hours before the evening service and a few minutes before he had to officiate at a friend's wedding, Bill laid his head down on his desk and sobbed uncontrollably, entirely depleted of physical, emotional, and spiritual strength. As he said later, "Something broke inside me that day. I didn't know what it was, but it scared me. I felt as if I were coming apart at the seams."[8]

A church of fifteen thousand, national recognition, and unparalleled ministry success—but still Bill Hybels was a victim of the dark side.

Victims Great and Small

If there is any consolation in all of these stories, it can only be that we are not alone in our struggle. Whether a beloved American president, an infamous world leader, a Fortune 500 executive, a servant-minded pastor of a country church, or an effective denominational leader, the dark side is indiscriminate when it comes to choosing its victims. Be they well-intentioned leaders or dictators driven by sinister motives, their dark side, like oil in a body of water, will always find its way to the surface and create a mess if it is not acknowledged and redeemed.

TARGETING INSIGHTS

- The dark side can be found in leaders throughout all eras.
- People who ignore or refuse to acknowledge their dark side frequently encounter major failures in their leadership responsibilities.
- Leaders who face their dark side and redeem it accomplish the most over the long run.

APPLYING INSIGHTS

Looking back over your lifetime, think of the leaders you most admire and those you least respect. To your knowledge how aware were they of their own dark side? How did they handle their dark side? Who was the most successful at it? What does all this mean for your own life and leadership role?

4

SHEDDING DIVINE LIGHT ON THE DARK SIDE

I f we are ever going to understand the sources and effects of our dark side well enough to overcome it and keep it from destroying our ability to lead for God's glory, we must seriously consider God's original design for us and the corruption of that design, which resulted from the very first leadership failure.

The First Leadership Failure

God's original intent for humanity was to exercise leadership in his created order:

> Let Us make man in Our image, according to Our likeness; and let them rule over the fish of the sea and over the birds of the sky and over the cattle and over all the earth, and over every creeping thing that creeps on the earth.
>
> Genesis 1:26

God originally placed human beings on the earth to serve as rulers. The Hebrew word for *rule* in Genesis 1:26 comes from the root word that means to exercise dominion. It was a word frequently used in the Old Testament in reference to Israel's ruling over other nations and being the source of authority and direction for them.[1] This rulership that God granted to Adam was not limited to merely the oversight of animal and plant life but extended to every living thing on the earth. Scripture records that God blessed Adam and Eve and said to them, "Be fruitful and multiply, and fill the earth, and subdue it; and rule over the fish of the sea and over the birds of the sky, and over *every living thing* that moves on the earth" (Gen. 1:28, emphasis ours).

Clearly God intended humans to be more than just managers. There is an implied sense that they were responsible to do the right things with the earth and all that was on and in it, the divine resource they had been given. Adam and Eve were responsible to see that life on earth was conducted as God would want it conducted had he been physically in charge himself. That is the role of leadership: to do the right things, not merely to do things right.[2]

Unfortunately that first experiment in human leadership did not end successfully. As with all leaders and the environments in which they lead, there were certain parameters placed on Adam and Eve. The parameters were established for their own protection, not simply to make their task more difficult. God's command was certain: "From any tree of the garden you may eat freely; but from the tree of the knowledge of good and evil you shall not eat, for in the day that you eat from it you will surely die" (Gen. 2:16–17).

Rather than remain content to exercise their considerable authority within God's established parameters, they chose to challenge those parameters.

The serpent said to the woman, "You surely will not die! For God knows that in the day you eat from it your eyes will be opened, and you will be like God, knowing good and evil." When the woman saw that the tree was good for food, and that it was a delight to the eyes, and that the tree was desirable to make one wise, she took from its fruit and ate; and she gave also to her husband with her, and he ate.

Genesis 3:4–6

The reason for this challenge to the parameters God had established was the need they felt to gain equal status with God. Simply put, the first human leadership failure was the result of unrestrained pride and selfishness with a healthy dose of self-deception. With several variations and minor additions, these provide the raw material for our dark side.

Raw Material for the Dark Side

There are many scriptural admonitions that warn us of our fallen human tendencies toward pride, selfishness, self-deception, and wrong motives.

Pride

Solomon, a leader who clearly struggled against his dark side, speaks with a measure of experience and personal insight when he writes, "When pride comes, then comes dishonor, but with the humble is wisdom" (Prov. 11:2). He also addressed the destructive nature of pride when he wrote, "Pride goes before destruction, and a haughty spirit before stumbling. It is better to be humble in spirit with the lowly, than to divide the spoil with the proud" (Prov. 16:18–19). Pride in Scripture is almost exclusively linked with failure and stumbling. It is one of the human traits about which God has expressly declared his hatred in Proverbs 6:16–18. "There are six things which the LORD hates, yes, seven which are an abomination to Him," and the first characteristic singled out in this infamous list is "haughty eyes" (pride) closely followed by another of our raw materials for the dark side, "a heart that devises wicked plans" (wrong motives). In fact so repulsive to God is the person swollen with pride that the writer of Proverbs also says that "everyone who is proud in heart is an abomination to the LORD" (Prov. 16:5). If these statements were not enough to convince us of the evil of pride, we're also told that "a man's pride will bring him low" (Prov. 29:23).

Though pride is without a doubt the foundation on which the dark side is built and extremely destructive when left unchecked, it is also an area that many Christian leaders ignore when it comes to accountability to others. The insidious nature of pride is such that Christian leaders believe they do not struggle with it. Or if they do, certainly not to the same extent that others do.

Pride seems to be one of the constant components of every human personality that irresistibly begins early in life to drive us. It is one of the elements of our dark side that Scripture indicates can cause serious difficulties not only in our exercise of leadership but also in our daily living. It can safely be said that pride is the primal sin. It was pride that caused Lucifer to challenge God's authority resulting in his rejection from heaven, thus creating the seeds that have germinated into all manner of human evil (Ezek. 28:17). But pride is not the only raw material used in the manufacture of our dark side.

Selfishness

If there is a close second to pride when it comes to our dark side, it is our all-consuming selfishness. We are born with a natural bent toward gratifying ourselves, and beginning with our hungry, demanding cries during infancy, that bent is to some degree reinforced throughout our early years of life. We learn as babies that all we must do to gratify our needs is to cry and someone will be there to satisfy us and stop the crying. Unfortunately it is a habit that is hard to break as we grow older.

Scripture tells us that selfishness, like pride, will end in our own disaster.

> But because of your stubbornness and unrepentant heart you are storing up wrath for yourself in the day of wrath and revelation of the righteous judgment of God, who will render to each person according to his deeds: to those who by perseverance in doing good seek for glory and honor and immortality, eternal life; but to those who are *selfishly ambitious* and do not obey the truth, but obey unrighteousness, wrath and indignation.
>
> Romans 2:5–8 (emphasis ours)

Though we are all aware of the selfishness underlying many of our choices, it is never easy to admit and is something we work hard as leaders to hide. Like a hungry shark being careful to keep its telltale dorsal fin just below the surface so as not to reveal its location to a potentially gratifying meal, we become adept at keeping our selfishness carefully submerged so as not to reveal our true motives. But just as the famished shark will eventually break the surface in an explosion of fins, blood, and boiling water, so selfishness will ultimately result in chaos in our leadership.

> But if you have bitter jealousy and selfish ambition in your heart, do not be arrogant and so lie against the truth. . . . For where jealousy and selfish ambition exist, there is disorder and every evil thing.
>
> James 3:14, 16

The disciples James and John experienced the disorder that selfishness can bring to the leader's relationships. Though they were handpicked for leadership by Jesus himself and were exposed to his perfect, selfless example, they were still overcome by selfishness.

> James and John, the two sons of Zebedee, came up to Jesus, saying, "Teacher, we want You to do for us whatever we ask of

You." And He said to them, "What do you want Me to do for you?" They said to Him, "Grant that we may sit, one on Your right and one on Your left, in Your glory."

Mark 10:35–37

On learning about James and John's selfish request for special consideration and recognition from Jesus, "the ten began to feel indignant with James and John" (v. 41). Selfish leaders always leave chaos and disorder in their wake.

It is natural to rationalize and hide our selfishness, but doing so only leads to trouble. We need to admit it and overcome it. As the apostle Paul says:

> Do nothing from selfishness or empty conceit, but with humility of mind regard one another as more important than yourselves; do not merely look out for your own personal interests, but also for the interests of others.

Philippians 2:3–4

Self-Deception and Wrong Motives

Solomon writes in Proverbs, "All the ways of a man are clean in his own sight, but the LORD weighs the motives" (Prov. 16:2). There seems to be a sense in which leaders can always justify their plans and goals as good and right. As human beings we have an inherent ability to deceive ourselves. Thus equipped we are capable of transforming even the most selfishly motivated action into an act of sacrificial altruism in our own minds. Jeremiah tells us, "The heart is more deceitful than all else and is desperately sick; who can understand it?" (Jer. 17:9). The clear answer to Jeremiah's rhetorical question is that no one can understand the treacherous dealings of the human heart. We cannot even fully understand our own heart and motives. The unhappy truth is that all too often we are not that interested in probing our motives too deeply for fear of what we might find.

62

The apostle Paul seems to agree with Jeremiah's assessment when he tells the Corinthians, people known for judging the motives of others:

> To me it is a very small thing that I may be examined by you, or by any human court; in fact, I do not even examine myself. For I am conscious of nothing against myself, yet I am not by this acquitted; but the one who examines me is the Lord.
>
> 1 Corinthians 4:3–4

Paul is not saying that he never engages in self-examination of his motives, but quite to the contrary, even though he examines himself and finds nothing against himself, this does not necessarily mean he is not guilty of wrong motives. Paul recognized that his heart was deceitful. Thus he would leave all final judgment up to the Lord.

Jesus himself said that it is out of our heart, or our inner being, that all sorts of deceptions and evil are born. Jesus on one occasion told his disciples:

> For from within, out of the heart of men, proceed the evil thoughts, fornications, thefts, murders, adulteries, deeds of coveting and wickedness, as well as deceit, sensuality, envy, slander, pride and foolishness.
>
> Mark 7:21–22

There is a comprehensive list of materials for the human dark side.

From a biblical perspective then, what does it look like when these raw materials are combined to form the dark side? What does the finished product look like?

The Raw Materials at Work

The Bible never covers up the sins of God's people. Contrary to what some expect, it exposes numerous leaders who experienced significant failure as the direct result of their dark side.

Saul

Saul experienced significant failure as a leader. His downfall was precipitated by his disobedience to God's clear commands regarding holy warfare. Saul thought that he was somehow above the need to wait for the prophet Samuel to make a sacrifice at Gilgal before going to war, and that arrogant attitude marked the beginning of the end of Saul's leadership. Saul continued in arrogance when he failed to obey the command to totally destroy Amalek. Again thinking he was somehow above the law, he decided it would be acceptable to disobey in a limited way (1 Samuel 9–15).

It was after these episodes of disobedience that his leadership of the nation was wrested from him. He was rejected by God as the leader of the people, God's Spirit was removed from him, and he began to experience severe bouts of anxiety, depression, and paranoia.[3] In the later stages of his leadership his paranoia became so consuming that it had a destructive impact not only on him, but also on his son Jonathan; on his imagined rival, David; and on the entire nation.

In Saul's personality and behavior we see signs of pride, selfishness, self-deception, personal insecurity, low self-worth, and extreme paranoia. Not even his selection by God, the gifting of God, or his natural ability was enough to neutralize the dark side of his personality. Paradoxically, Saul's initial humility, in spite of his being extremely handsome and gifted, no doubt contributed to God's selection of him as the nation's leader and to his initial effectiveness. And yet in the end what made him great—his special call and his ability—conspired against him to cause his failure. He began to believe that he was above God's laws and the obedience required of others. Though the life and leadership of Saul provide an interesting biblical case study in the dangers of the dark side, he is by no means its only victim.

David

King David also periodically battled with his dark side, resulting in humiliating personal defeats and devastating national consequences. His pride as a leader caused him to take a census of his warriors in direct violation of God's command, leading to the needless death of many innocent people. His selfishness consumed him as he committed adultery with Bathsheba, murdered her husband, and then deceived himself as he covered up his sin for nearly a year until he was finally confronted by Nathan the prophet (2 Samuel 11–12; 24).

However, in spite of his frequent battles with the dark side, it seems that David was aware of his dark side and was willing to deal honestly with himself before God. After his pride-generated numbering of his warriors and the tragedy that resulted, the Scripture records, "Now David's heart troubled him after he had numbered the people. So David said to the LORD, 'I have sinned greatly in what I have done. But now, O LORD, please take away the iniquity of Your servant, for I have acted very foolishly'" (2 Sam. 24:10).

We also see indications of David's self-awareness and corrective action in Psalms 32 and 51. But in spite of the fact that David did not experience failure on the same scale as Saul, his dark side did lead to failures that had far-reaching effects on himself, his extended family, and the nation.

In addition to Saul and David there are numerous other biblical leaders who waged war against their dark side. The evidence would seem to indicate that Solomon struggled against a narcissistic personality[4] and Moses seems to have battled a compulsive personality.[5] Both of these biblical leaders also suffered negative consequences as a direct result of their dark side getting the upper hand in the exercise of their leadership. There are numerous other leaders throughout the Scriptures who struggled in similar ways with the dark side of their personality, some more successfully than others.

Light That Brings Understanding

Even with this very limited amount of scriptural light being shed on the human dark side, it becomes even clearer that anyone who aspires to leadership, particularly spiritual leadership, needs to become fully aware of the raw materials that go into the creation of the leader's dark side and how those have been mingled during the course of his or her lifetime with issues from the family of origin, personal experiences, and a unique personality to create his or her dark side. This understanding is necessary to be able to take defensive measures to prevent the dark side from causing significant leadership failure.

How do pride, selfishness, self-deception, and wrong motives combine with our personality and life experiences to manufacture our dark side? What are the signs of its presence in our life and leadership? It is to these questions we now turn our attention.

TARGETING INSIGHTS

- The human dark side is rooted in the beginning of history as recorded in Genesis 1–3. Pride, selfishness, self-deception, and wrong motives are the raw materials of which the dark side consists.
- The fall of many leaders described in the Bible is directly attributable to components of their dark side. Because of the providence of God, some leaders do at times carry out their leadership responsibilities in spite of their dark side.
- Leaders who are aware of their dark side and are willing to deal openly and honestly with it before God are empowered for greater effectiveness.

APPLYING INSIGHTS

Do you identify more with Saul or with David? In what ways do you see yourself in each of them? Is your approach to your own dark side more like Saul's or David's? What would you like your approach to be in the future?

5

HOW THE
DARK SIDE
DEVELOPS

A s we have seen in the previous chapter, contrary to much contemporary thought, every leader possesses within him or her the raw material necessary for the manufacture of the dark side. None of us are immune. We are not, as some would suggest, "whole" at birth, only to be tainted by cultural and sociological influences as we experience life.[1] But rather, we all enter life with the same primal baggage just waiting to be unpacked, hung on the hangers of our life experiences, and finally placed in the closet that is our dark side. The issue is not so much whether or not anyone is immune to the effects of the dark side, but what it is that causes every leader to be affected differently. What allows some leaders to lead for a lifetime relatively unscathed while others meet with devastating failures? For example, Jim Bakker and Bill Hybels have both struggled with the dark side in the exercise of their leadership but have experienced completely different results; one a humiliating failure, the other significant, seemingly balanced success. Though every leader must do battle with pride, selfishness, self-deception, and wrong motives, what is it that causes some leaders to stumble so tragically, while others are able to maintain their balance and keep these primal forces in check?

Without doubt, much of what determines how a leader's dark side will develop, as well as how he or she will deal with that dark side once in leadership, stems from the family the person grew up in and his or her childhood years through adolescence. As we grow toward adulthood, our dark side begins to develop silently, only to emerge fully at some future date, often after leadership has been attained. As author Robert A. Johnson says: ". . . somewhere early on our way, we eat one of the wonderful fruits of the tree of knowledge, things separate into good and evil, and we begin the shadow-making process; we divide our lives."[2]

The critical factor in how our dark side will impact our leadership is the extent to which we learn about its development and understand how it influences us. If it is true that each of us will develop a shadow, or dark side, then what are the signs of its presence in our life?

Signs of Our Shadow Side

Though we may not be aware of its presence, we have been impacted by the dark side throughout our life. There are definite signs we can become sensitive to that will help us identify the unique ways it has developed over the years as well as the specific shape it has taken in our life. Often we are conscious of these signs in our motivations and recognize their influence on our behavior, yet we are not quite able to make a solid connection between them and their source.

Many of us in positions of leadership or aspiring to leadership have sensed at one time or another a vague, inexplicable drive to make a significant mark with our lives. At times we can even begin to describe what it is we are driven to achieve. But a complete description always seems to elude us, and we just continue to be pulled along by this unidentified but powerful force toward some ultimate goal of which we are not completely aware. This vague sense of ambition is a sign that our dark side is alive and well. But there are others.

Some leaders experience a profound need to be approved by those they lead and to know that they are accepted and appreciated. This is not just the ordinary, normal desire we all possess to be liked by others but rather a desperate, almost life-sustaining need to gain approval. It is another sign that the "shadow-making" process, as Robert Johnson refers to it, has taken place.

For others it may be an irrational fear that their work is not adequate, so they are driven to work even harder and longer to prevent their irrational fear from becoming a reality. A symptom of the dark side for others may be a need to feel in absolute control of every circumstance and event. This need to be in control often extends beyond the workplace and into family life and relationships, becoming a need to control other people. A tendency toward perfectionism and many other behaviors such as overeating, compulsive spending, alcoholism, and compulsive exercise are all signals that should be explored.

In short any behavior that seems to overpower us, as well as any urge or motivation that seems to uncontrollably drive us, is a possible sign indicating the presence of our dark side. How do these inner urges and compulsions develop to such a point? The shadow-making process is not a solo act; it is truly a family affair.

A Family Affair

If pride, selfishness, self-deceit, and wrong motives are the crucial ingredients in the recipe for our dark side, then our family—and our developmental years in that family—most certainly provides the catalyst for this mixture that determines the final shape our dark side will take. With rare exception the experiences of our childhood determine the degree to which we are controlled by the dark side of our personality and how it manifests itself when it comes to the exercise of leadership. This is true of even the most popular and powerful leaders.

One of the most idealized leaders of the twentieth century was John F. Kennedy. After a rapid rise through the ranks of Congress he was elected to the most powerful position of leadership in the world at an amazingly early age. He launched the United States on a quest to conquer the final frontier of space, set the pace at the beginning of the Cold War, and left an indelible mark on the American psyche. Yet for all of his achievements, John Kennedy was driven by his dark side. It has only been since his death, after decades of research into previously unavailable documents, that the American public has learned to what extent this was true.

John Fitzgerald Kennedy was born to Joseph P. and Rose Kennedy, the second of nine children. The Kennedy family provided young John with an environment in which his dark side would not only develop but also flourish and be encouraged. Clare Boothe Luce, wife of the famous publishing magnate Henry Luce, once described the Kennedy family as one in which there was "ambition and pride and human wreckage, such dedication to the best and lapses into the mire of life; such vulgar, noble, driven, generous, self-centered, loving, suspicious, devious, honorable, vulnerable, indomitable people."[3]

The greatest influence on the young president's life was his father. He was a powerful and wealthy man yet one who never thought he had completely arrived at the high station he deserved in life, always feeling the outsider in Boston high society. Though he had achieved great success from a material standpoint, it was not enough. As a result of this low self-image, which bordered on paranoia, he was determined to find his greater success and acceptance through the lives and successes of his sons. In an effort to guarantee that his sons succeed and provide him with the level of social acceptance he so desperately needed, Joe Kennedy created an environment that fostered sibling competition—the winners were rewarded with paternal affection. In fact the primary motivation throughout much of the sons' lives was gaining the approval of their father. "What mattered most to the four sons, in their early years, was their competition for the love and applause of their father."[4]

In addition to the need young John felt to gain his father's approval, which was never easily won, there were other formative influences at work in his childhood. His father was a known adulterer, often maintaining sordid relationships with numerous women, even defiantly flaunting them before his wife and family. Once young John Kennedy got stuck on the family sailboat as his father was leaving for a sail with movie star Gloria Swanson, one of his mistresses. John hid himself below deck only to peek out from his hiding place to see his father engaged in sexual relations with the young starlet. He was so horrified by what he saw, he jumped overboard and started swimming out to sea.[5] Joe encouraged his sons to demonstrate their manhood in the same way he did. Illicit sex was never frowned on but encouraged as a badge of power and virility. The sons even provided young women for their father's pleasure and on many occasions shared the women with him.

But those were not the only influences that were seminal in the shaping of Kennedy's dark side. There were also the lessons of winning at any cost, tailoring the truth to one's own advantage, and the privileges of money and power. These among numerous other influences created a dark side to John Kennedy's personality. His entire adult life was nothing more than a veiled quest for his father's approval, from his need to achieve during his school years to his rapid ascent up the ladder of political power.

Once he attained the ultimate position of power, his dark side became evident to those around him. As president, he too flaunted his adulterous affairs before his wife.[6] Had his term not been cut short by tragedy, it is likely that his dark side would eventually have created serious problems for him, the Prince of Camelot. One political insider said, "The whole dark side of John Kennedy wouldn't emerge until after his death. . . . We had hints of it; we saw it around the edges. . . . Then we began to see it. You just connected the dots, and there was a picture there."[7]

The Needs That Drive Us

As in the case of John F. Kennedy, there are experiences and influences during our childhood and adolescent years that combine with the primal raw materials present in each of us to develop our dark side. Though each of our family backgrounds and experiences are different, we have common needs and wants that make us vulnerable to events that threaten us in some way. These events cause us to respond to our different formative experiences in different ways that ultimately produce our unique dark side.

A Pyramid of Needs

The concept of the hierarchy of needs, developed by Abraham Maslow, is familiar to most leaders who have taken an introductory psychology course, but fewer leaders are aware of the significant role this familiar concept plays in the development of their dark side.

Maslow postulated that every person operates on the basis of a pyramid of needs and wants. This pyramid of needs is arranged hierarchically, ranging from basic physiological needs at the base to safety needs, needs for affection and belonging, the need for esteem, and ultimately the need for self-actualization.[8] Maslow's thesis is that people must have their needs met at one level of this pyramid before they will move on to satisfy their needs at a higher level.

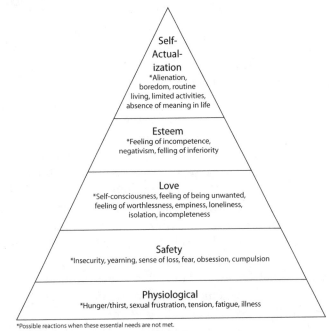

Self-Actual-ization
*Alienation, boredom, routine living, limited activities, absence of meaning in life

Esteem
*Feeling of incompetence, negativism, felling of inferiority

Love
*Self-consciousness, feeling of being unwanted, feeling of worthlessness, empiness, loneliness, isolation, incompleteness

Safety
*Insecurity, yearning, sense of loss, fear, obsession, cumpulsion

Physiological
*Hunger/thirst, sexual frustration, tension, fatigue, illness

*Possible reactions when these essential needs are not met.

Figure 1

This quest to satisfy our needs ends only with death. It is not a static process but rather one that is quite dynamic. For example, it is possible to have our basic needs for safety met for a period of time, but that does not mean those needs are satisfied for life. There may come a time when we experience some tragedy or event that threatens our feelings of safety and causes us to revert for a time to a lower level on the pyramid. This can be a real event that we experience firsthand, or it can be a tragedy that has happened to someone else to whom we feel close. Reading about an assault or murder in the neighborhood where we live is one of those events that can cause our safety need to be threatened even though the attack did not happen directly to us. When we feel unsafe, we revert to that level of need from a higher one.

Missing Blocks in Our Pyramid

As Maslow's pyramid graphically demonstrates, we all have essential needs that must be met. As children and adolescents we do not spend much time contemplating the fulfillment of these needs; it is essentially a subconscious process.[9] And yet the satisfaction of these needs is vital to our healthy development. What happens when some of these most basic needs are never adequately satisfied? Worse yet, what happens when we experience some traumatic event during our childhood or developmental years that causes us to feel permanently threatened in one of these essential areas, even though that level of need might be satisfied in many other respects? When this happens, we end up with missing blocks in our need pyramid that we will attempt to meet, often subconsciously. This is the heart of how our dark side begins to develop.

When certain events threaten us in one of our need areas or when we are deprived in any way, we should expect meeting that need to become a controlling element of our personality. If threatening events and unmet needs are acknowledged and dealt with openly, meeting the needs can be a healthy process. If, however, we perceive our attempts to meet these unsatisfied needs as a sign of weakness or personal failure or if we are unaware of how to meet these needs, our attempts are often sublimated and begin forming what will become our dark side.

Our need for safety is one of our most basic needs. What happens when we as a child or young adolescent experience abandonment by a parent or the loss of a parent through death? Though we may not be able to adequately process the full impact of that loss on our psyche, we know it would definitely threaten our safety needs. Unless we have an incredibly healthy family support system that is able to offset our sense of abandonment and reassure us in our need to feel secure, our loss will leave us with a missing block in our need pyramid that we will either consciously or subconsciously attempt to satisfy. Because we cannot regain our lost parent, our efforts to fill in the missing block will likely be redirected to areas that we may be better able to control. For example, we may engage in an endless search for safe and protective people or environments. Though this may seem overly simplistic, it actually happens in many areas of our lives.

A significant number of leaders of the past and present came from rigid homes with unrealistic standards and a perfectionistic parent who withheld approval and signs of love until those perfect standards were attained. This type of environment threatens the need that children have to feel approved and accepted by the most important people in their life—their parents. This withholding of love or lack of demonstrable approval by a parent for whatever reason creates a deep hole within the personality of the child and may launch him or her on a life quest to gain the approval of that parent. Leaders too numerous to mention here, in virtually every field of endeavor, are engaged in a silent and probably subconscious attempt to satisfy their need to gain the approval and acceptance of a parent. Unfortunately, even as these driven leaders are applauded and rewarded for their achievements, because the need that drives them is so deeply embedded and has not even been identified by them, they continue to be obsessively driven to achieve still more.

This same process occurs with virtually any type of unmet need. How many adults today are impacted by unmet needs resulting from a childhood spent in an alcoholic home or a family where physical and emotional abuse took place? Though these individuals are no doubt aware of the dysfunctions that existed in their family system (though some continue in denial all of their lives), it is less likely that they are able to make the direct connection between that family experience and their pyramid of needs. If, however, a connection can be made, these individuals will be better able to understand how certain of those needs, having not been satisfied, result in the development of their dark side—a dark side that will have a significant influence in the course they chart through adulthood.

A Debt We Cannot Pay

Another important element in the development of our dark side is what is labeled "existential debts,"[10] the belief that our unmet need is our fault and we must somehow satisfy it. An existential debt is created in our life as the result of a particularly traumatic event, again usually experienced in childhood. When parents divorce, for example, often children experience the failure of the parents' relationship as a personal failure. They quietly blame themselves for the failure of their parents' marriage: *If I had been more obedient,* they think; *If I had kept my room clean maybe Dad wouldn't have left our house,* they reason. However, because the children were not in reality the cause of the marital split, there is nothing they can do to resolve the problem and compensate for their imagined role in the divorce. It is a debt they feel they owe but one they can never repay since it exists only as a result of their immature reasoning process.

When people feel they owe an existential debt of this nature, it is a powerful contributing factor in the development of their dark side. In many instances their entire adult life will be spent in a subconscious effort to repay the debt. Obviously they believe the more significant their activities and accomplishments are as an adult, the greater the likelihood of repaying the debt.

The great Indian leader Mohandas Gandhi is an example of a highly successful leader who went through life experiencing an existential debt. When he was a very young teenager he was married as the result of a prearranged betrothal. He found that he looked forward with great anticipation to the sexual passion the evenings would hold for him and his young bride. At this same time his father was deathly ill and Mohandas would spend hours by his father's bedside gently nursing him and providing him with much needed company. On one occasion, after having sat with his father for numerous hours, he was relieved in his vigil by an uncle. Having been relieved of his duties, he was only too anxious to go straight to his marital bed and enjoy the company of his wife. Shortly after having entered his room with his wife, news came that his father had died just moments after he had left. The young Gandhi was gripped by a terrible sense of guilt; he felt that his father had died as a direct result of his lust.[11] This experience created an existential debt in Gandhi's life and had a profound impact on the development of his dark side, thus greatly influencing his style of leadership. His lifelong obsession with nonviolent reform was a subconscious attempt to repay this existential debt.

A Pattern Emerges

As one begins to study the development of the dark side, a clear pattern begins to emerge, a pattern that involves four specific stages as shown in the following chart:

Stage	Basic Element of That Stage	Explanation of Stage
Stage One	Needs	The existence of basic needs (see Maslow's need pyramid)
Stage Two	Traumatic experiences	A traumatic experience that threatens the satisfaction of certain needs or leaves us with unmet needs resulting in a "missing block" in our pyramid of needs
Stage Three	Existential debt	The feeling that our unmet need is the result of a personal failure, which creates an emotional debt that we attempt to pay through often unhealthy behaviors during our adult years
Stage Four	Dark side development	The combined effects of these needs, traumatic experiences, and emotional debts result in the ongoing development of our dark side

Now let's take this model and plug in a more concrete example so that we are able to see how the dark side begins to develop in our lives.

As we have seen, we all have a deep need to feel accepted, particularly by those individuals we consider most important in our lives. For Christians this would obviously include God as well as our parents. Let's see how Sam's experiences fit into our model according to the stages we have identified.

Stage One—Needs: One of the needs in Sam's pyramid was to feel approved and accepted by God. Since his early experience taught that God's approval would be expressed through the baptism in the Spirit and the ability to speak in other tongues, this is what he sought.

Stage Two—Traumatic experiences: On many occasions at summer camps and special revival meetings the speakers communicated that God longed to give this gift of Spirit baptism to anyone who wanted it. The highlight of these special meetings was the reception of this coveted gift by seemingly everyone in attendance who had not yet received it. Try as he would, Sam was never able to experience this great blessing. These were traumatic experiences that threatened his deep need to feel approved and accepted by God and resulted in a missing block in his need pyramid.

Stage Three—Existential debt: These traumatic experiences created what for many years was an existential debt that Sam felt he needed to pay. He thought the only possible reason he had not been able to receive the gift of the Spirit like everyone else was because he had done something very wrong. Sam believed for most of his teen years that the reason God had not given him this ultimate stamp of approval was because he had committed the unpardonable sin. That is a pretty serious debt to be faced with as a teenager.

Stage Four—Dark side development: This existential debt resulted in a frantic search for God's approval and blessing and a subconscious attempt to pay this debt. What better way to pay this debt than to enter full-time Christian service? Certainly

God would have to smile on Sam then. However, because the debt was so great, he was driven to achieve exceptional success, which eventually led to his emotional explosion described earlier. This is simply an example of how one event, combined with other dynamics—such as Sam's need to please and his tendency toward perfectionism as modeled by his father, as well as the raw materials of his fallen human nature—work together to produce the dark side.

Though the pattern seems clear as presented here, much of what took place during those years was at a subconscious level. For many years Sam could not even begin to identify the process that was taking place in his life and fueling his need to succeed in ministry at all costs. Sam was simply carried along by these powerful forces, only aware of one thing: no measure of achievement was bringing the fulfillment and sense of accomplishment that he had hoped it would. The success he was craving was synonymous with and essential to receiving God's approval and finally satisfying the unmet need, which in turn would indicate that his debt had finally been paid.

This drive to succeed had at times resulted in behavior and practices as a leader that may have left many innocent and silent victims.

In fairness it needs to be stated that there are many people who have possibly been brought up in the same religious environment as Sam was and also were not able to experience the baptism in the Spirit, yet it did not affect them in the same way. We are all unique individuals, thus our dark side will be unique to us. Yet regardless of the shape our dark side eventually takes, the process will be similar once we are able to step back and identify it.

Same Pattern but Different Dark Sides

For each of us the particulars will be different, but the basic process will be essentially the same. For some it might be an alcoholic parent or physical abuse during childhood that will need to be plugged in the model above. For others it may be a perfectionistic parent or a humiliating experience suffered at the hands of other children. Being left out of the popular social group while in high school or being turned down by the first person you ever asked out for a date may have had a tremendous impact. But whatever it is that you find yourself plugging into those categories in the chart, it has almost assuredly led to the development of your dark side. When those experiences and influences are combined with the raw materials of pride, selfishness, self-deception, and wrong motives, we can begin to see how our dark side develops into such a powerful, controlling influence in our lives and leadership.

A Good Side to the Dark Side?

Is it possible that there is any good that can come of our dark side? The encouraging answer to that question is yes! As we saw in the case of Gandhi and will see in the next chapter, our dark side can to a certain extent propel us to attempt and accomplish things we might not have otherwise attempted apart from its presence in our lives.

TARGETING INSIGHTS

- The dark side of leadership develops through a predictable pattern even though the particulars will be different for each person. With rare exception the experiences of our childhood and adolescence form our dark side.
- Though we may be only subconsciously aware of our dark side, there are signals that point to it. Such signals are observable in a drive to succeed, desire to be accepted, irrational fear, need to be in control, perfectionism, or various compulsions.

- Our dark side is inclined to be an overcompensation for needs that have not been met in our lives and develops as we attempt to repay the existential debts of varying degrees that we have taken on.

APPLYING INSIGHTS

What are the experiences from your past that formed your own dark side? How do these past experiences show up in observable ways today? In what ways do they prove to be helps and/or hindrances to your leadership?

6

Seafood, Pictionary, and the Dark Side

For many leaders, entrepreneurs, and successful business-people, the dark side has provided the fuel for achievement necessary to set them apart. Though often it can be a painful and debilitating force in our lives, our dark side can also serve as a silent internal mentor, tirelessly coaching us to triumph in the same areas of our lives that helped create it. In virtually every field of endeavor, leaders have knowingly and unknowingly ridden the wave of their dark side to astounding success.

The Making of a Seafood Success

"Son, you don't weigh enough to play this game!" The words landed on the ears of the eager thirteen-year-old with devastating and humiliating force. As he rode his bike home from the practice field that day, his eyes were flooded with tears of disappointment and shame. For Garry Loncon this seemingly benign episode, played out on an adolescent field of dreams, would provide the seeds for the dark side that would motivate him and influence his choices into adulthood.

As a young boy Garry was always small for his age. In spite of his scanty physical stature he had developed a passion for athletic competition. His older brother was a gifted athlete in both football and baseball. Garry's father was a former Golden Gloves boxer and coached the Pee Wee baseball teams on which Garry and his brothers played. These family examples fueled the fires of Garry's competitive spirit. In the seventh grade Garry felt certain he could win a spot on his neighborhood Junior National football team with his sure-handed catches and quick, darting pass routes perfected during countless hours of sandlot contests. So when he stepped on the scale that day on the practice field, the coach shattered his dream. He felt inferior to the other boys and as if he were destined to be second string all of his life. Maybe he would never become a starter.

Rather than defeating him, this traumatic rejection became a life-shaping catalyst that drove Garry to prove he could compete and succeed. Though he was never able to compete as a starter, he still found a way to participate in athletics and rub shoulders with the star athletes he admired and secretly longed to be. As a result of his obvious desire to be a team player and contribute to the success of the team, one of Garry's high school coaches, now the offensive coordinator for the University of Washington's football team, invited him to become a team manager. It was an invitation he eagerly accepted. But Garry was not content being just a manager. He was determined to become an athletic trainer, an even more respected position in the eyes of the athletes. Once he achieved the status of trainer, Garry was determined to become the best trainer in the history of the high school, a lofty goal he was also able to achieve. Because of his high level of excellence and determination to become the best, Garry won a college scholarship to Western Washington University as a varsity athletic trainer.

Today Garry Loncon is no longer a second-string player. At thirty-eight he is the chief executive officer and a partner in Seattle-based Royal Aleutian Seafood, Inc., one of the fastest growing producers and distributors of crab in the highly competitive seafood industry. With annual revenues in excess of fifty million dollars, Garry has led Royal Aleutian from troubled financial waters to solid profitability within four years of his joining the company in 1992. In addition he has led the seafood producer to impressive gains in market share each of the years he has been with the company. From its position as a perennial bit player in the crab business, Royal Aleutian's market share has risen sharply to third nationally, surpassed only by industry giants Peter Pan and Trident Seafood. These are impressive achievements for a kid who had fears of never getting off the bench and into the game. But Garry's success is not uncommon for those who are driven by the dark side.

The Dark Side of Pictionary

Millions of people have had hours of enjoyment with friends and family playing the board game Pictionary. But few if any know that it owes its existence at least in part to the dark side. Rob Angel, the creator of Pictionary, has experienced phenomenal success by anyone's standard. Today Rob is aware that much of the success he enjoys was nurtured and took root in the soil provided by his dark side.

Born in the pristine province of British Columbia, Canada, Rob spent his early childhood living in the shadows of the majestic Canadian Rockies. Before he began his formal schooling, Rob's family moved to Washington State. Though the family's move changed little in terms of geography, there were subtle, unseen changes in dialect and culture lost on a boy of five or six. Once settled in their new community, Rob's parents enrolled him in first grade at the local elementary school. Because classes had already begun, the young Canadian joined his new classmates on a day when a spelling test was to be given, a test for which Rob was totally unprepared. Though he gave it his best effort, the result was a disaster. Thirty-two years later, comfortably seated in his spacious and luxurious Seattle home, Rob distinctly recalls the teacher's glaring at him when the papers were passed back and then with clear disapproval in her voice saying loudly enough for the entire class to hear, "You don't know how to spell at all!" That experience, harmless as it may seem, left a powerful imprint on his six-year-old mind that still influences him. "To this day," Rob says, "I see myself as a poor student and just average academically."

Whether the teacher's words were spoken with contempt or simply offered as remedial observation cannot be determined. What matters is the impact they had on a young boy who clearly did not interpret them as encouraging or supportive. They were received as painful verbal blows that left invisible bruises on a young, insecure boy. Rob felt as if he had been publicly singled out as a failure. It was this simple childhood event that planted the first seed of Rob's dark side.

In light of Rob's difficulty with words in first grade, it is interesting that Rob has gained international fame and tremendous wealth as the creator of a board game that uses pictures to communicate words. One of Rob's most memorable and painful childhood experiences has been redeemed by the worldwide success of a word game.

Obviously one such event in the life of a child is not necessarily enough to become a driving force for success. Garry Loncon's failure on the football field and Rob Angel's flunked spelling test alone are not sufficient to explain their almost obsessive determination to succeed. But when combined with other, similar experiences and the raw materials in a personality, the dark side begins to operate in earnest.

Sticks and Stones

"Dirty Jewish pig!" Just a few short years after his spelling test embarrassment, this racist epithet, hurled by thoughtless schoolmates on a childhood playground, pierced Rob's already tender psyche.

Being a young Jewish boy in an overwhelmingly Waspish city, which had only one synagogue for a population of two hundred thousand residents, was not an ego-building experience. However, it did provide a tight-knit, family feeling for the relatively small Jewish population. As a result, Rob learned early in life how to compensate for his minority status with a charming, outgoing personality that won him many high school and college friends and still serves him well. But the stain of hurtful words carelessly blotted across the porous canvas of a young life is not easily erased. These experiences and others began to fuel Rob's inner fire and provide the drive that would one day propel him to a level of success he might otherwise never have achieved.

Education and a Working Mom

While Rob Angel had his share of struggles in the school environment, Garry Loncon, in contrast, found in academia a field on which he could finally compete with even the most gifted.

Garry's father, whom Garry had elevated to hero status, felt a sense of failure for never having gained a formal education and frequently gave verbal expression to his feelings of failure. Consequently Garry and his brothers were encouraged to make the most of their education.

Even while in grade school Garry had determined that he would help ease his father's sense of shame by becoming the first member of his extended family to graduate from college. Once in college, however, Garry was not content merely to graduate; Garry graduated with honors.

Another of the more traumatic and motivating events in Garry's development was learning that his mother, a gracious, strong, and attractive woman, was working as a maid for the families of his wealthier high school classmates. Garry describes it as a personal epiphany of sorts that deeply impacted him, serving to reinforce his feelings of inferiority.

For Garry, the ingredients that went into the creation of his dark side would ordinarily be considered harmless: a slight physical stature that foiled his athletic aspirations, a greatly admired father who felt shame because of his own lack of education, the realization that his mother was cleaning the homes of his schoolmates, and the material deprivations that generally accompany a working-class upbringing. All of these early childhood and adolescent experiences left Garry with a missing block or two in his pyramid of needs, particularly the love and esteem blocks. He didn't feel the acceptance of the star athletes he so admired and he felt like he was second string. Those feelings generated the need to succeed as well as the need for the acceptance and approval that would attend that success. As Garry put it, "I felt I had something to prove. To whom I don't really know; maybe I wanted to impress the athletes I looked up to." He adds, "I wanted to prove to my parents and friends that I could excel in something." Though he could never quite identify the feelings and needs that were beginning to bubble inside his life, they propelled him to achieve the success he now enjoys.

Today Garry is finally understanding his dark side. He now realizes that his considerable success will not erase the childhood experiences that have driven him. Though they might be quieted somewhat by his achievements, they are still there, just beneath the surface, motivating him to maintain his newfound role as a starter.

For Garry Loncon continued success will require that he manage his childhood feelings of inferiority and the fear of failure. He will need to learn when enough success is enough and that no amount of money or achievement will ever completely eradicate the memories and feelings he carries with him today. For, all too often, when the lessons of the dark side are never learned, it drives even successful leaders to make unwise, impulsive, unethical, or immoral choices that may ultimately lead to the forfeiture of the very success it has created.

Sibling Rivalry and a Disappointing Victory

The journey for Rob Angel, though different from that of Garry Loncon in the specifics, has nonetheless been charted to some degree by the dark side.

Rob remembers being in constant competition with his older brother for the attention of his parents. His brother, Harvey, was a natural comedian who kept the family constantly laughing and cast a long shadow over Rob's life. One of the most disappointing episodes in Rob's adolescence was when he thought he had finally outperformed Harvey. Jewish boys study hard to perform well at their bar mitzvah, a very important rite of passage. For this important occasion Harvey failed to apply himself, and the result was a good but uninspired bar mitzvah. Rob saw it as the opening he had been awaiting. He determined to excel at his bar mitzvah a few years later and steal away the limelight that Harvey seemed to constantly occupy. Rob executed his plan flawlessly. He studied hard, practiced his Hebrew, and shone brightly at his bar mitzvah. Of course he expected his parents to be very happy with his performance and looked forward to the family picture-taking ritual that would immortalize his hard-earned victory over Harvey. It didn't come. In fact a picture was never taken. This was not an intentional oversight on the part of Rob's parents and they did congratulate him on his achievement, but at the same time, the lack of photos Rob had anticipated was to him a significant omission. It was a source of great disappointment that still feeds Rob's dark side. He continues to feel driven to match his previous success by creating

91

another game and by developing Pictionary into a syndicated television game show.

Shedding Light on the Dangers of the Dark Side

Both Garry and Rob have grown in awareness of their unique dark side. They have taken time to reflect on the powerful influence their dark side has played in their current success. But overcoming the negative aspects of the dark side requires continued vigilance. Like all successful leaders, Garry and Rob will need to understand that the powerful forces that helped forge their success can also facilitate their failure.

TARGETING INSIGHTS

- There is a good side to the dark side. It often serves as a silent mentor, tirelessly coaching us to triumph in the same areas of our life that helped create it in the first place.
- Those who reflect will see that the dark side has a powerful influence on their current success.

APPLYING INSIGHTS

After reading the stories of Garry and Rob, write a similar story about yourself. Reflect on your past and describe how your dark side directed your life, career, and ministry.

7

PARADOXES
OF THE
DARK SIDE

Few events have gripped the collective albeit lurid interest of our nation like the Jim Bakker-PTL scandal of the late 1980s.[1] For months *Nightline*, the popular ABC news program hosted by Ted Koppel, featured the main characters in that tragic drama as well as biting commentary. At the heart of Jim Bakker's fall from grace were violations of federal laws regarding wire and mail fraud. In an effort to advance his PTL kingdom Bakker frequently solicited donations for specific projects but used the funds for whatever project he was most interested in at the time. The promises of lifetime partnerships that would provide free stays at Bakker's Christian "Disneyland" in return for the sacrificial gifts of his television congregation never quite materialized as advertised.

A strong subplot to the drama involved the now infamous New York church secretary Jessica Hahn and a sordid tryst in a Clearwater, Florida, hotel room with Jim Bakker and several of his associates. In an effort to keep the now-sullied secretary from speaking to the press, Bakker authorized a financial pay-off. The entire fiasco was brought to the public's attention by another televangelist, Jimmy Swaggart, whose sole motivation, so he said, was to protect the integrity of television ministry and maintain purity in the body of Christ. Swaggart was himself exposed not long afterward as a frequent visitor of prostitutes, resulting in his own tearful confession and the ultimate downsizing of his television empire.

What role did the dark side play in the tragic fall of Jim Bakker? Was he simply a sophisticated spiritual charlatan, scheming from the beginning to bilk people out of millions of dollars to finance a frivolous and extravagant lifestyle? Or could it be that Jim Bakker launched his energetic ministry with the most noble of intentions, only to find himself unwittingly overtaken by his own dark side? In the life and ministry of Jim Bakker we can see a very clear example of both the potential and problems, what we might call the paradox, of the dark side as it relates to the exercise of leadership.

An Ache to Achieve

As early as the late 1950s a youthful Jim Bakker had aspirations to make his mark in ministry.[2] He longed to make a mark in just about anything that would get him a little attention. In fairness to the aspiring young minister, his desire to make a difference was not a conscious attempt to elevate and promote himself. He had a genuine desire to see the gospel proclaimed and people brought to new life in Jesus Christ. However, from his earliest years the seeds of the dark side had been deeply planted in his developing personality as the result of what he perceived to be an underprivileged childhood. According to Jim, his family "lived in poverty" in Muskegon, Michigan, and he was "embarrassed about [his] family's house." He says,

"Whenever someone drove me home from school, I'd ask to be dropped off several blocks away so they wouldn't see the house."[3] He also cringed at the lack of sophistication displayed by his Pentecostal church and the frugal, clearly second-class way in which the church building was maintained. The pastor of his home church would paint Sunday school classrooms purple simply because the paint was free. This was a source of embarrassment to the young Bakker.

Jim Bakker's record as a student only reinforced his sense of self-depreciation. He had such poor grades as a high school senior he was not able to graduate with his class and was forced to repeat his senior year.[4] Later, his television parishioners didn't know that their TV "pastor" never graduated from North Central Bible College, even though he implied that he had.

Another source of the future televangelist's low self-image was his slight physical stature. As a college student he weighed only 130 pounds and had a diminutive presence.

Bakker received little affirmation or encouragement from his parents. His mother was cold and self-involved while his father was stern, judgmental, hardworking, and tight with what little money the family had.[5] Clearly one of the most traumatic events in Jim Bakker's life was the personal failure of his older brother, Bob, during Jim's teenage years. Bob's drinking and carousing caused the family great embarrassment. Bakker recognized the scar his brother's behavior left on the family and he determined to step into the place of honor vacated by his brother in an effort to ease the family pain. This was one of the earliest signs of his developing dark side: an attempt to feel better about himself and boost his low self-image, even if it was at the expense of his fallen brother.

Because of his deeply rooted feelings of inferiority, Jim Bakker had an ache to achieve and prove to himself as well as others that he would not be a failure like his brother Bob. Though he had a knack for entertaining and loved the spotlight, he knew that Broadway was an unlikely avenue for attaining the achievement he longed for, and it was certainly taboo in his Pentecostal church environment. The road of the traveling evangelist offered a quicker, more acceptable route to success. Being an evangelist provided a profession with the public exposure he longed for and in which his level of achievement would only be hindered by his own lack of effort, something that would never be a problem for the eager Bakker.

Jim Bakker achieved amazing success by anyone's standards. At the time of his fall Bakker was the king of an impressive kingdom: the Heritage U.S.A. Christian theme park, the frontier-style Heritage Village housing complex, the Heritage Grand Hotel, the PTL water park, the high-rise Heritage Tower Hotel, Heritage Village Church, and a massive state-of-the-art television complex. Unfortunately, because he was unaware of his dark side, the seeds that had been sown began to grow wildly out of control until they finally produced their dark harvest. In the end the elements that motivated him to achieve his success also produced the self-deception and personal weakness that brought about his failure.

Driven to Fail

Not only did Jim Bakker's dark side create within him an ache to achieve in an effort to overcome his feelings of inferiority and low self-worth, but it also drove him to tragic failure. The nature of his unique dark side created a leader who saw no problem with accepting exorbitant six-figure bonuses even as the ministry was deeply in debt. His extravagant lifestyle served as a constant salve that was generously applied to his fragile self-image in an effort to quiet that constant whisper in his ear. Biographer Charles E. Shepard says, "His ready access to PTL cash and credit cards fostered a lifestyle that dimmed his exaggerated memories of threadbare coats and an orange house on Sanford Avenue."[6]

Though it was no doubt a subconscious reality, PTL was not primarily God's vehicle for reaching people but rather an extension of Jim Bakker's personality. PTL *was* Jim Bakker. Consequently any attempt to rein in the growth and out-of-control finances at PTL was synonymous with preventing its psychologically needy leader from achieving what defined him as a person. Without his constant involvement in substantial projects, each more magnificent and grand than the one before, Jim Bakker saw himself as a puny Bible school dropout, living on the wrong side of the tracks in working-class Muskegon, an image he had spent all his life trying to erase. It was a self-image he could not live with, even if it meant his ultimate self-destruction.

This personal flaw, a product of his dark side, was the greatest contributing factor to his failure as a leader. Though his dark side provided the drive, perseverance, and savvy that enabled him to build a massive Christian organization, it also prevented him from seeing his own flaws and taking the proactive steps that could have countered them and resulted in even more effective, but balanced, leadership. In the final analysis, had Jim Bakker taken the time to engage in serious self-examination, receive honest feedback from those who knew him, and learn about his dark side, he might still be the head of PTL. He could have identified some of the negative effects of his dark side, submitted himself to accountable relationships, and put in place protective organizational structures that might possibly have prevented such a tragic fall.

Such is the paradoxical nature of the leader's dark side. It is not the exclusive nemesis of nationally known leaders and popular televangelists. It is common to every individual who is in or aspires to leadership. How easy and natural it is for us to sit back in self-righteous judgment of the Jim Bakkers and Jimmy Swaggarts of the Christian world, while even as we cast our stones, we ignore the same principle at work in our own leadership. Tragic failures like that of Jim Bakker are found every day in churches across America, albeit on a smaller scale, as pastors and Christian leaders experience everything from serious moral failures and unethical behavior to simply dropping out of ministry altogether because their dark side makes them incapable of doing their work. It does not have to be this way.

A Power for Good

World-famous evangelist Billy Graham is an example of a leader who was motivated to achieve as the result of a traumatic experience during his teenage years but who has avoided becoming a victim of his dark side. At the age of eighteen Billy fell hopelessly in love with a young girl by the name of Emily and proposed marriage. After months of hesitating to give him an answer, Emily finally accepted Billy's proposal of marriage. He was ecstatic! However, several months later Emily broke off the engagement and returned the high school ring he had given her. Billy was staggered by the blow. In a letter to his friend Wendell Phillips, Billy wrote, "All the stars have fallen out of my sky. . . . There is nothing to live for. We have broken up." Billy's sister Catherine described the broken engagement as "definitely traumatic," and she felt it caused him to be driven to greater seriousness. Billy's brother Melvin gave a different assessment of the situation: "She wanted to marry a man that was going to amount to something, and she didn't think he was going to make it. I will never forget that. We figured she was right. It so broke him up. I think it was a big turning point."[7]

It was this traumatic event of losing the girl he loved because of insufficient promise that may have caused Billy to aspire to do "something big," as he put it. He became highly motivated to prove Emily and his family wrong and make something of himself. Though this rejection created a deep inner wound (a missing block in his need pyramid) and drove him to achieve, God obviously worked through it. It might have been just what the tall, skinny, frequently ill Billy needed to motivate him to attempt things he might not otherwise have attempted.

Over the years Billy Graham has been attentive to the shadowy workings of his dark side. During his rise to international leadership and fame his self-awareness grew in equal measure. Billy Graham became a leader who was also a student of himself and understood the areas of his dark side that made him vulnerable to temptation and he took proactive steps to prevent his becoming a victim of the dark side. Early in his ministry at a Modesto, California, hotel room, he called his ministry associates together and said:

> God has brought us this far. . . . Maybe He is preparing us for something that we don't know. Let's try to recall all of the things that have been a stumbling block and a hindrance to evangelists in years past, and let's come back together in an hour and talk about it and pray about it and ask God to guard us from them.[8]

In spite of the fame he has received, Billy Graham has maintained a sterling reputation and enhanced the cause of Christ in untold ways. God was able to use Billy's dark side because of Billy's willingness to understand his weaknesses and continually seek God's protection and guidance.

Learning to Understand Our Dark Side

When our drive to achieve, fueled by unmet needs (e.g., the need for approval) and existential debt, is channeled in the right direction, it can be a power for good. However, when that need-fueled drive becomes misdirected, it can result in disaster as we have seen. The key that will determine whether we experience success or tragic failure is the degree to which we become acquainted with our dark side and put in place the defenses that will prevent it from running rampant and trampling our ability to lead effectively.

As we grow in leadership, we will experience failures, tension, emotional struggles, interpersonal conflicts, and other events that can expose our dark side to us if we are attentive. Over time we should begin to understand the experiences that have been foundational in the development of our dark side and begin to search for the tools that will prevent it from causing us to derail.

The various characteristics of the dark side can be grouped into some broad categories, which are discussed in part 2. Even though these five categories may not account for every possible related issue we face, they can provide the general framework we need to begin the process of understanding our unique dark side.

TARGETING INSIGHTS

- The dark side can spawn good or bad, joy or pain, potential or problems.
- The negative aspect of the dark side rises to the surface when we use it selfishly to only fulfill our own needs and wants.
- We can use our dark side to serve God's purposes in our life rather than only our unmet needs.

APPLYING INSIGHTS

Contemplate the paradox of the dark side in your own life. Where have you seen it surface in a negative manner? How does it serve God's purposes in your life?

PART 2

DISCOVERING OUR DARK SIDE

8

THE
COMPULSIVE
LEADER

As an infant, tragic circumstances dictated that the young boy be abandoned by his parents. This severe measure, reluctantly taken by his parents, was the only hope the child had for survival. It was done in an effort to save his life.[1] Unfortunately, children cannot understand the circumstances or discern the motivations that precipitate such traumatic events. They are simply left to spend a lifetime sorting through and dealing with the emotional debris that inevitably results.

Growing up, it probably was not too difficult for the boy to figure out that he was an adopted child. He looked different from his adopted family and was from an entirely different culture. He probably asked the same questions every adopted child eventually asks: Why? What was wrong with me? Why didn't my parents want to keep me? These questions are often a lifetime in the answering.

As the boy grew and matured he learned of his cultural heritage and likely began to understand more about the circumstances that led to his abandonment as an infant. However, simply understanding does not remove the scars, or the pain.

When he was a young man, it had become clear to him that members of his own race and culture were living in an oppressive state. As a result of having been adopted into a wealthy, well-connected family, the young man now had the power and position needed to bring liberation to those from his race who were still suffering as political prisoners and slaves. However, his initial attempt to liberate his people resulted in failure. In fact it resulted in murder. When his adoptive grandfather learned of this subversive act, he took steps to have his adopted grandson killed to pay for the crime. The young man fled to a foreign country to save his life (Exod. 2:1–15).

Such were the childhood experiences of Moses. Abandonment by his parents as an infant, adoption by the enemies of his own people, an upbringing in the rigid environment of a royal family with the accompanying high expectations, a significant failure, and the ultimate rejection by his adoptive grandfather comprised Moses' formative years. It no doubt was the combination of the unmet needs stemming from this childhood that created Moses' dark side and resulted in his becoming a compulsive leader.

Moses: A Man in Control

At the time Moses led the Israelites from their Egyptian bondage, conservative estimates place the number of people under his leadership at around three million. During any age and for any leader, no matter how gifted, this is an impossible number of people over which to exercise direct control. And yet it appears from the biblical record that Moses felt a need to have control and believed that he alone was capable of doing the job correctly. In Exodus 18 we are told that Moses alone would mediate disputes among the people and render authoritative judgments. In order to accomplish this task the people with disputes would stand around Moses from "morning until evening," a period of at least twelve hours, so that Moses could settle their problems. Apparently some of these disputes were quite petty in nature (Exod. 18:22).

One would think that a man with Moses' level of education and his exposure in Egypt to the most sophisticated form of government known to the world at that time would see the need for delegating authority. But it took his shepherd father-in-law, Jethro, to witness this inefficient practice and suggest organizational changes before Moses could see that his compulsive need to control was not healthy for him or the people (Exod. 18:17–18).

In addition to the control issue it would seem that Moses was subject to occasional public eruptions of anger. In fact one of his public outbursts resulted in his being forbidden to enter the Promised Land, the ultimate purpose of his leading the people out of Egypt (Num. 20:1–13). Although any analysis of Moses' personality can only be conjecture, it would seem reasonable to assume that his public outbursts of anger in the face of difficult people may indicate some repressed anger and resentment from his early years.

In spite of Moses' struggles God used him in amazing ways to advance his kingdom plan, and he enjoyed close fellowship with God (Deut. 34:10). Whatever the exact cause, in the life and leadership of Moses we can see some of the signs of the compulsive leader.

Maintaining Control at All Costs

Compulsive in a leadership context describes the need to maintain absolute order. Because compulsive leadership results from the leader's own compulsive personality, the leader sees the organization as another area of his life that must be controlled. The leader sees the organization's performance as a direct reflection of his or her own person and performance. The compulsive leader pursues perfection to an extreme, both in personal and organizational life. Compulsive leaders generally develop very rigid, highly systematized daily routines that they must follow meticulously.[2] These can involve exercise, devotions, schedule, and family routines and extend into the leadership of organizations.

Compulsive leaders also tend to be very status conscious and as a result are deferential and ingratiating with their superiors, often going out of their way to impress them with their diligence and efficiency.[3] They continually look for the reassurance and approval of authority figures and are anxious when unsure of their performance and standing.[4] Because all of these efforts require an enormous amount of energy, compulsive leaders are excessively devoted to work, often becoming workaholics. They work inordinate hours to the detriment of their family and establish an unhealthy example and environment for staff members. Staff then feel like slackers if they don't keep up with the boss or if they want to leave the office after a normal day's work. There is little room for spontaneity, and even compulsive leaders' recreation and pleasure are often planned in advance so as to get the most out of their relaxation time. These leaders are often overly moralistic, conscientious, and judgmental both of themselves and others.[5]

Although compulsive leaders are pictures of absolute order (e.g., their grooming, clothing, speech, family, and work environment), on the inside they are an emotional powder keg.[6] At heart they can be angry, rebellious individuals who believe it wrong to express their true feelings. These feelings can be the result of a rigid childhood where unrealistic expectations were placed on them. Or they can be the product of some failure or childhood trauma to which they were not allowed to give appropriate expression. Whatever the source, compulsive leaders respond to their inner turmoil by so tightly binding their feelings that the opposite of turmoil results—highly controlled and ordered individuals.[7] This is why it is common for such persons' repressed anger to be expressed in sudden and violent outbursts, only to be just as quickly controlled, with appropriate apologies extended.

Ultimately all attempts to exercise and maintain control of their lives and environments are efforts to keep repressed anger, resentment, and rebellion from surfacing. It is not unusual for compulsive leaders to have so deeply buried this anger, living in denial for such an extended period, that they are unaware of its presence. The first step toward regaining balance is to identify whether compulsive leadership is a problem and then begin reflecting on the possible sources.

Compulsive Leaders in the Church

There are many pastors and spiritual leaders today who feel the need to be in complete control of their organization in every minute detail. They must oversee the preparation of the bulletin to ensure it meets their high standards. They pick every song for Sunday worship. There is a worship director, but that person cannot match the song perfectly to the theme of the sermon. These leaders are obsessive over every decision. One pastor of a large church insisted that his staff wear black or blue suits, white shirts, and red ties. This was staff policy!

Compulsivity in the church often shows up in the pursuit of excellence in ministry. This striving for excellence can become perfectionism. Compulsive leaders see the organization they lead as an extension and reflection of themselves. Therefore, any flaws in the organization are seen as a direct reflection on them personally. We firmly support excellence in ministry, but there must be balance. We need to recognize when our pursuit of excellence is crossing the line to obsessive perfectionism. Excessive criticism and critiquing can be another symptom of compulsive leadership in the church. Very often such leaders are most critical of themselves, but their attitude affects others within the organization.

Though all of the above behaviors are done under the guise of serving God and doing our best for the Lord, which is very

107

admirable, in reality it is all done in an attempt to meet and satisfy the leader's unhealthy needs.

TARGETING INSIGHTS

- One manifestation of the dark side is the development of the compulsive leader. Moses is one example found in the Bible.

- Some signs of a compulsive leader include the following: Compulsive leaders are status conscious, looking for reassurance and approval from those in authority. They try to control activities and keep order and usually are workaholics. At times they are excessively moralistic, conscientious, and judgmental.

- At heart compulsive leaders have an angry and rebellious attitude. Since they may not feel it is proper to express their true feelings, they may repress their anger and resentment.

APPLYING INSIGHTS

How do you know if you are a compulsive leader? If you have read to this point and cannot identify with anything that's been said, you probably are not a compulsive leader. If, however, you caught brief glimpses of yourself in some but not all of the signs described, you might have some tendencies toward being a compulsive leader. Then there are those of you who felt as if someone had climbed inside your skin and described you perfectly. You are most likely a compulsive leader.

To help you understand if this is the shape your dark side has taken, we offer the following inventory. Read each statement and circle the number that corresponds closest to your impressions about yourself.

1 = strongly disagree   2 = disagree   3 = uncertain   4 = agree   5 = strongly agree

1. I often worry that my superiors do not approve of the quality of my work.   1 2 3 4 5

2. I am highly regimented in my daily personal routines such as exercise schedule or spiritual disciplines.   1 2 3 4 5

3. When circumstances dictate that I must interrupt my daily personal routines, I find myself feeling out of sorts and even guilty for having "skipped" a day.   1 2 3 4 5

4. I frequently find myself conscious of my status in relationship to others.   1 2 3 4 5

5. It is difficult for me to take an unplanned day off from work responsibilities just to goof around or spend time with friends or family, feeling like a "slacker" if I do.   1 2 3 4 5

6. While away from work, I still find myself thinking about work-related topics, often sitting down to write out my ideas at length, even if it disrupts family activities.   1 2 3 4 5

7. I like to plan the details of my vacations so I don't waste time or miss anything important.   1 2 3 4 5

8. I often explode in anger after being cut off while driving or after being irritated by other petty issues.   1 2 3 4 5

9. I am meticulous with my personal appearance, keeping shoes shined, clothes perfectly pressed, hair carefully cut and groomed, and fingernails clipped.   1 2 3 4 5

10. I frequently comment about the long hours I keep and my heavy workload but am secretly proud of my "work ethic."   1 2 3 4 5

11. When another person makes sloppy errors or pays little attention to detail, I become annoyed and judge him or her.   1 2 3 4 5

12. I am obsessive about the smallest errors, worrying that they will reflect poorly on me.   1 2 3 4 5

Add up the circled numbers and place the total here: _____

If your total comes to less than 20, you probably are not compulsive. If your total is between 21 and 40, there is a likelihood that you have *some* compulsive tendencies. If your total is 41 or more, you probably are a compulsive leader.

Do you see the traits of a compulsive leader in yourself? In what ways does this type of leader mirror your dark side?

9

THE NARCISSISTIC LEADER

Ancient Greek mythology tells the story of a young boy by the name of Narcissus. Narcissus was a beautiful boy. So beautiful, the fable has it, that his face appeared to be chiseled from the most perfect marble and his neck looked as smooth as unblemished ivory. Because of his extraordinary beauty, many of his peers were attracted to him but none could get through to him. They reached out to Narcissus and extended their love to him, but he was not interested in any of them; he had found his love interest closer to home. At the age of sixteen Narcissus was walking along the mythical river Styx when he approached a calm pool of water to get a drink. As he moved his face closer, he saw his own image reflected in the pool and was transfixed. From that moment on Narcissus was in love with the image he saw reflected in that riverside pool—his own image. Because he was so obsessed with his own image, he could not love anyone or return anyone's love. As the story goes, Narcissus eventually could not bear to leave his reflection in the pool. He lay down by the pool and pined for himself until he finally was absorbed by the earth and became a flower—the narcissus, which can still be found on the banks of most ponds, its reflection glimmering in the water.[1]

Solomon: A Man Obsessed with His Image

It is never easy to follow a legend. Whenever a new leader is faced with the task of filling a beloved and successful leader's shoes, it is almost always an uncomfortable fit. That is especially true when the new leader happens to be the son of the living legend being replaced. Such was the predicament of Solomon.

For forty years King David ruled as a benevolent king and was greatly loved by his people. His accomplishments and reputation were bigger than life: war hero, expander of the nation, a handsome and gifted king. But as with all beloved and legendary leaders, the torch must eventually be passed to the next generation. Enter Solomon.

Solomon's transition to this challenging position was not without its problems. Solomon ascended to the throne in the midst of much family tension. When King David was on his deathbed, his eldest son, Adonijah, assumed that he would naturally ascend to the throne and declared himself king over Israel. However, because he knew that Solomon was his father's favored son, he did not invite Solomon, Solomon's mother Bathsheba, or David's trusted advisor, Nathan the prophet, to his coronation festivities. On learning of Adonijah's bold move, Bathsheba and Nathan hatched a plan to usurp the throne from him and install Solomon in his place. As a result Solomon became king at the urging of his mother under less than ideal circumstances—a fact that surely was not lost on the young prince.

Solomon was quite young and inexperienced in political matters (1 Chron. 29:1). It is probably safe to assume that Solomon's contrived route to the throne, his youthfulness and inexperience, the legendary success of his father, as well as his probable awareness of the circumstances of his own birth that followed the death of David and Bathsheba's child born of adultery all combined to provide a sense of inferiority and a powerful drive within the young king to make a name for himself.

Because of the legacy of his father, David, Solomon would always be looking over his shoulder; simply succeeding would never be enough for an insecure young king. Making a name for himself would require doing something grand. Even with the prospect of building the great temple (plans and preparations for which had already been made by his father), there was always the possibility of failure. Or worse yet, what if people attributed the temple's completion to David's planning and preparation? Whatever the reasons, Solomon hatched plans for his kingdom on a scale previously unheard of in Israel.

> I enlarged my works: I built houses for myself, I planted vineyards for myself; I made gardens and parks for myself, and I planted in them all kinds of fruit trees; I made ponds of water for myself from which to irrigate a forest of growing trees. I bought male and female slaves and I had homeborn slaves. Also I possessed flocks and herds larger than all who preceded me in Jerusalem. Also, I collected for myself silver and gold and the treasure of kings and provinces. I provided for myself male and female singers and the pleasures of men—many concubines.
>
> Ecclesiastes 2:4–8

Even with a cursory reading of Solomon's project list it is easy to recognize the focus of all his efforts—himself! With the constant refrain of me, mine, and myself, King Solomon reveals that he is obsessed with himself and with creating an image that would outshine the star of his revered father, David. Apparently he succeeded, at least for a while. As a result of his massive, self-indulgent projects he began to feel temporarily satisfied with the image he had created for himself.

> Then I became great and increased more than all who preceded me in Jerusalem. My wisdom also stood by me. And all that my eyes desired I did not refuse them. I did not withhold my heart from any pleasure, for my heart was pleased because of all my labor and this was my reward for all my labor.
>
> Ecclesiastes 2:9–10

It would seem that Solomon, the tentative young king who got off to a troubled start, had more than just a healthy self-image. He had become bigger than life in his own mind. But this world-class greatness was not without significant cost. To fund his desires, Solomon taxed the people to the point of economic exhaustion. When image is everything, no price is too high—especially when it is being paid by others.

In addition to the misappropriation of national financial resources, Solomon was willing to tarnish the integrity of his office by violating divine mandates in an effort to advance himself. In Deuteronomy there were three specific prohibitions for whoever would serve as king over God's people: the king should not multiply horses for himself (especially not horses from Egypt), he should not multiply wives for himself (lest they turn his heart away from devotion to the Lord), and he should not increase silver and gold for himself (Deut. 17:16–17). Evidently Solomon's obsession with his own image was so overpowering that he blatantly violated each of these prohibitions. Yet in spite of it all, Solomon could not find the satisfaction and meaning he had hoped his grand achievements would produce. Instead they led him to this life-shaking midlife encounter with the dark side.

When Image Is Everything

For the narcissistic leader, such as Solomon, the world revolves on the axis of self, and all other people and issues closely orbit them as they get caught in the strong gravitational pull of the narcissist's self-absorption. As seen in the life of Solomon, narcissistic leaders "present various combinations of intense ambitiousness, grandiose fantasies, feelings of inferiority and overdependence on external admiration and acclaim."[2] At the same time the self-absorbed leader is chronically uncertain of himself and experiences dissatisfaction with his accomplishments, which he tries to overcome by exploiting others in ways that will help elevate his self-image.[3] In addition, narcissistic leaders have an overinflated sense of their importance to the organization and an exhibitionistic need for constant attention and admiration from others, especially those they lead and any person or group to whom they report. In spite of their drive to achieve greatness, their restless ambition is rarely satisfied in a way that enables them to enjoy their accomplishments. Another characteristic is their "interpersonal exploitiveness, in which others are taken advantage of in order to indulge [their] own desires or for self-aggrandizement."[4] Solomon displayed this type of behavior through overtaxing the people in an effort to finance his own self-promoting projects.

Narcissistic leaders also tend to overestimate their own achievements and abilities while stubbornly refusing to recognize the quality and value of the same in others. Any recognition of someone else's accomplishments or abilities is a threat to their own self-importance and risks the loss of the exclusive admiration they crave from their followers. Because narcissistic leaders tend to use others to advance their own goals, they are notorious for being unable to empathize with those they lead. This enables them to pursue their own ends without restraint. Though narcissism seems to be diametrically opposed to the concept of spiritual, servant leadership, it is all too common in the church and among spiritual leadership.

Narcissistic Spiritual Leaders

So how do narcissistic leaders show up in the church and Christian organizations? Though it may not be on the same scale as Solomon, Christian leaders often use those they lead to enhance their own image and improve the way they feel about themselves. Far too many sermons are preached in an effort to gain the approval and admiration of followers, with little or no concern for God's approval. The pastor or speaker who steps down from the platform and is immediately obsessed with whether his sermon was good is dealing with a prime symptom of narcissism.

Jim Bakker seems to have been a classic victim of narcissistic personality disorder.[5] His visions of grandeur were born out of deep feelings of inferiority and inadequacy. He was driven to achieve in an effort to prove to himself and others that he was worthy and approved. So deeply rooted was his psychological need to achieve greatness that he would stop at virtually nothing in an effort to gain the approval and recognition he craved.

Numerous churches have been destroyed by leaders who led the church into projects too energetic and costly for the congregation because the leader needed to feel good about himself. How easy it is for Christian leaders to use their organizations as nothing more than platforms from which they launch themselves on their chosen career path with little or no regard for the long-term health of the organization they were entrusted to lead.

When a pastor or Christian executive says to himself, This church (or organization) would suffer if I ever left, it is a sign of narcissism. When the leader is constantly beginning new ministries, even when existing, essential ministries are not adequately staffed or effective, it is a sign of narcissism. Rather than ensuring that existing ministries are efficiently functioning, the narcissistic leader needs the kudos that come from new and unique ministries. However, once the "high" of a new ministry

116

launch is gone, the narcissistic leader provides little long-term oversight or maintenance.

Because ministry provides the ready justification that grandiose visions and risky ventures are necessary to accomplish God's kingdom work, the church and Christian organizations provide fertile soil for budding narcissists. Tragically, because many followers of the narcissistic leader think all this activity is being done for God, they feel uncomfortable challenging their leader.

TARGETING INSIGHTS

- One manifestation of the dark side is the development of the narcissistic leader. Solomon is one example found in the Bible.
- Some signs of a narcissistic leader include the following: Narcissistic leaders are driven to succeed by a need for admiration and acclaim. They may have an overinflated sense of importance as well as great ambitions and grandiose fantasies.
- At the heart of narcissistic leaders are self-absorption and uncertainty due to deep feelings of inferiority. In addition, they may not enjoy their success and may be dissatisfied with their lives.

APPLYING INSIGHTS

So how do you know if you are narcissistic when it comes to the exercise of leadership? Chances are that you who battle these issues were uncomfortably aware of it as you read this chapter. However, one of the traits of narcissistic leaders is that they live in a state of constant denial and self-justification. Therefore, the following inventory may be helpful.

1 = strongly disagree   2 = disagree   3 = uncertain   4 = agree   5 = strongly agree

1. Fellow leaders in my church or organization frequently question whether my proposed goals and projects are feasible and realistic.   1   2   3   4   5

2. I am obsessed with knowing how others feel about my performance.   1   2   3   4   5

3. I find it difficult to receive criticism of any kind, reacting with anger, anxiety, or even depression when it does come.   1   2   3   4   5

4. At times I find myself thinking, I'll show them; they could never make it around here without me, when I experience conflict situations or opposition to my proposals and plans.   1   2   3   4   5

5. In spite of achieving what others would consider significant success, I still find myself dissatisfied and driven to achieve greater things in an effort to feel good about myself.   1   2   3   4   5

6. I am willing to bend rules and press the envelope of acceptable behavior to accomplish my goals.   1   2   3   4   5

7. Deep down I find myself feeling jealous of the success and achievements of associates or organizations in my area or field of expertise.   1   2   3   4   5

8. I am often unaware of or unconcerned about the financial pressures my goals and projects place on those I lead, my family, or the organization I serve.   1   2   3   4   5

9. Success or failure in a project has a direct bearing on my self-image and sense of personal worth.   1   2   3   4   5

10. I am highly conscious of how colleagues and those to whom I am accountable regard my accomplishments.   1   2   3   4   5

11. I need to be recognized or "on top" when meeting with a group of fellow leaders or associates.   1   2   3   4   5

12. I see myself as a nationally known figure at some time in the future or have plans to attain such a position.   1   2   3   4   5

Add up the circled numbers and place the total here: _____

If your total comes to less than 20, you probably are not narcissistic. If your total is between 21 and 40, there is a likelihood that you have *some* narcissistic tendencies. If your total is 41 or more, you probably are a narcissistic leader.

Do you see the traits of a narcissistic leader in yourself? In what ways does this type of leader mirror your dark side?

10

THE
PARANOID
LEADER

I t is likely that history will not be kind to Richard M. Nixon. Though he was a man of incredible intelligence, resilience, and determination, his leadership was sabotaged by his own insidious dark side. No amount of political acumen or international-relations savvy could overcome the powerful influence of this tragic leader's dark side.

Richard Nixon was a man controlled by acute paranoia. He was highly suspicious of others—even his own staff members—and was obsessed with gathering information on perceived enemies that could be used to mount counterattacks against any and all adversaries. Even in the face of obvious wrongdoing Nixon refused to admit any failures or accept any blame. He was a master of denial. Had he learned about his dark side and become aware of the shape it had taken, he could have doubtlessly avoided the humiliation of Watergate and possibly salvaged his presidency. Instead he became one of this century's most prominent victims of the dark side. Richard Nixon was simply one link in an age-old chain of paranoid leaders who have destroyed themselves.

Saul: A Man Shackled by Suspicion

When Saul made his entrance on the stage of national leadership he was equipped for success. He was attractive and exceptionally gifted. He was appointed by God, who supernaturally changed him so that he could be an effective leader.

> Then the Spirit of the LORD will come upon you mightily, and you shall prophesy with them and be changed into another man. . . . Then it happened when he [Saul] turned his back to leave Samuel, God changed his heart.
>
> 1 Samuel 10:6, 9

Where it says that God changed Saul's heart in verse 9, the Hebrew literally says that God replaced his heart with another heart, a heart that would enable him to lead the nation. All of this was quite surprising to Saul, as he possessed a very low view of himself and the family from which he came. This sense of personal insecurity and low self-worth is evident in 1 Samuel 15:17 when Samuel rebukes Saul by saying, "Is it not true, though you were little in your own eyes, you were made the head of the tribes of Israel?" The idea of serving as the king of Israel was definitely foreign to the future Saul had planned for himself. Yet Saul was to be an instrument of service in God's hands.

When Saul was publicly crowned as king, there was a pocket of people who doubted that this "nobody" could liberate the nation (1 Sam. 10:27). Though Saul was aware of their pessimism, he did not defend himself or respond to his detractors. Unfortunately that would be the last time Saul took such a mature approach to his opponents, whether real or imagined.

The primary service that God had planned for Saul was the liberation of Israel from the oppression of the Philistines. Initially Saul gained the upper hand over the Philistines. But it was not long before Saul's dark side began to subvert his leadership and the plans that God had for it.

There are always parameters and restrictions on leadership. No leader, including Saul, has carte blanche. One of the restrictions on Israelite royalty was never to usurp the role of the priest. Before one important battle, as Saul waited for Samuel the priest to arrive and make the appropriate sacrifices, the people became restless and began to scatter. Saul was so concerned about this potential mutiny that he decided to make the priestly sacrifice himself. Moments after Saul made the sacrifice, which he knew was strictly prohibited, Samuel arrived on the scene and confronted Saul with his obvious disobedience to God's law. Saul justified his actions as necessary and refused to admit any wrongdoing (1 Sam. 13:11–13). It would prove to be the first baby step down the path of self-destruction for King Saul.

Shortly after this failure, Samuel announced that God had chosen to remove the mantle of leadership from Saul and had already chosen a new king, who would emerge at some time in the future. From that time, Saul's leadership was marred by suspicion, distrust of those around him, including close family members, attempts to coerce loyalty, and even spying. One particularly bizarre episode involved a time when King Saul prohibited his people from eating until he successfully avenged himself on his enemies (1 Sam. 14:24–30). In fact Saul said that anyone who ate before he gave the okay would be cursed. It was an extreme measure born of severe paranoia and deep distrust. In response to his father's command Jonathan said, "My father has troubled the land." Confusing Saul's plan was the fact that Jonathan, not knowing of the prohibition, was the first to violate the king's command. Interpreting his son's actions as treasonous, Saul intended to execute Jonathan for his crime. In God's providence the people rescued Jonathan from his father

(1 Sam. 14:31–45). After this Saul began a rapid descent into the depths of obsessive paranoia.

After yet another failure, when Saul failed to utterly destroy Amalek and refused to acknowledge any disobedience, a young shepherd by the name of David began to complicate Saul's life even further.

Well into his reign as king, Saul had still not accomplished his primary, divinely assigned task to deliver Israel from the Philistines. Israel was still being taunted by the Philistine giant, Goliath. David, the teenage shepherd, instantly won the hearts of the Israelites when he stepped forward and with one smooth stone destroyed the enemy giant.

As Saul traveled the land after Goliath's death, he heard women singing in the streets, "Saul has slain his thousands, and David his ten thousands" (1 Sam. 18:7). From then on Saul suspected David of trying to steal his throne. Saul said, "They have ascribed to David ten thousands, but to me they have ascribed thousands. Now what more can he have but the kingdom?" (1 Sam. 18:8).

Saul became afraid of David's popularity with the people. Here was a king, appointed by God himself and supernaturally gifted for the job yet jealous and suspicious of an inexperienced, teenage shepherd. Saul attempted to kill David on numerous occasions. When murder didn't work, Saul attempted to buy David's loyalty by giving him his eldest daughter in marriage. Regardless of what he tried, Saul could not quell his irrational fears and suspicions. Consequently he engaged in further acts of deception and spying in an effort to remove David from the kingdom. Ultimately Saul's neurotic activities led to his own breakdown and tragic failure. Such is the fate of the paranoid leader.

Afraid of Their Own Shadow

Like suspicious King Saul, paranoid leaders are desperately afraid of anything or anyone, whether real or imagined, they perceive to have even the remotest potential of undermining their leadership and stealing away the limelight. They are characteristically suspicious, hostile, and guarded in their relationships with others—even close associates and family members.[1] Like Saul, paranoid leaders are hypersensitive to the actions and reactions of those they lead, always fearful of potential rebellions. Because they are deeply insecure in their own abilities, paranoid leaders are pathologically jealous of other gifted people.

Like Richard Nixon, paranoid leaders use clandestine scheming and spying to maintain a firm grip on leadership. Often this takes the form of building secret alliances and networks with those who can be easily manipulated and impressed by the leader's position and power. Anyone who is thought to be a threat often finds himself or herself unwittingly caught in a web of misinformation and rumor spun by the paranoid leader and his or her network of spies and supporters.

Paranoid leaders may overreact to even the mildest forms of criticism. This is because the criticism of followers and colleagues is often thought to be an effort to overthrow them or diminish their power. In addition paranoid leaders are constantly attaching subversive meanings and motives to even the most innocent actions of others in the organization.[2]

Because of their suspicions, paranoid leaders will often create rigid structures and systems of control within their organization that enable them to keep their finger in every piece of the organizational pie and limit the autonomy of underlings and associates. Excessive staff meetings and reporting are often the result of this need to keep close tabs on those around them. Unfortunately, contemporary Sauls are sprinkled throughout the ranks of spiritual leadership.

Paranoid Spiritual Leaders

Today it is not uncommon to hear a pastor jokingly say, "I'd never let my board meet without me there." More often than many spiritual leaders would care to admit, it is no joke. For some pastors, their chief adversary is the governing board that ironically is supposed to be their chief partner in caring for the flock of God. But somehow, often as a result of a pastor's own insecurity, an adversarial relationship develops. To be fair, this fear is not always entirely without merit. What pastor has not heard the stories about the board that calls a special meeting while the pastor is on vacation—when the pastor returns from his summer break, a pink slip is on his desk. We both have friends who had this very thing done to them. In one instance it occurred after little more than one rocky year at a rural church where the relationships were too close and there were no personal boundaries. But it is the exception that an innocent, unsuspecting pastor is removed in this way.

Much more common in church ministry is the senior pastor who refuses to allow an associate to preach for fear the congregation might like the associate's preaching better than his own. Other times, when an associate is allowed to preach and he or she receives the approval of parishioners, a subtle jealousy grips the senior pastor and he begins to take steps to limit the praise the associate receives, usually by limiting his or her public exposure. And when a paranoid pastor enters the boardroom and finds even one board member who appears to be angry or frustrated, he immediately worries that the anger or frustration is directed toward him.

Another struggle for paranoid spiritual leaders is difficulty in developing and maintaining close relationships with members of their church or organization. Close relationships are difficult because they require a measure of self-disclosure and transparency that they worry could be used against them at some point to undermine their leadership. Such leaders believe it is better to maintain a safe distance from people even if it means being seen as aloof and uncaring. For the paranoid pastor the possibility of being unseated is not worth the risk inherent in intimate, accountable relationships.

Targeting Insights

- One manifestation of the dark side is the development of the paranoid leader. Saul is one example found in the Bible.
- Some signs of a paranoid leader include the following: Paranoid leaders are suspicious, hostile, fearful, and jealous. Afraid that someone will undermine their leadership, they are hypersensitive to the actions of others, attach subjective meaning to motives, and create rigid structures for control.
- At the heart of the paranoid leader are strong feelings of insecurity and a lack of confidence.

Applying Insights

Having read this chapter, do you wonder if you are a paranoid leader?

If so, the following inventory may provide you with some insight.

Read each statement and circle the number that corresponds closest to your impressions about yourself.

1 = strongly disagree   2 = disagree   3 = uncertain   4 = agree   5 = strongly agree

1. When I see two key leaders of my organization discreetly talking, I worry that they may be talking about me.   1 2 3 4 5

2. It really bothers me to think about my board or leadership team meeting without me being present.   1 2 3 4 5

3. When an associate receives rave reviews for a project or some special assignment, I experience intense jealousy rather than joy in the success and recognition he or she is receiving.   1 2 3 4 5

4. I require subordinates and associates within my organization to provide me with detailed reports of their activities.   1 2 3 4 5

5. I struggle when an associate, rather than me, is asked to take on a high-profile special assignment or project.   1 2 3 4 5

6. I have few intimate or meaningful relationships within my church or organization and find myself avoiding such relationships.   1 2 3 4 5

125

7. I insist on absolute loyalty from those who work for me and prohibit staff from criticizing me in any way.   1 2 3 4 5

8. I often worry that there is a significant faction within my organization that would like to see me leave.   1 2 3 4 5

9. I have probed people for what they know or for special information they may have relating to certain leaders in my organization.   1 2 3 4 5

10. Those I work with often complain about my lack of a healthy sense of humor.   1 2 3 4 5

11. I routinely refer to those I lead as "my people" or "my organization," yet bristle when the same designation is spoken by an associate.   1 2 3 4 5

12. I tend to take seriously even lighthearted comments and jokes directed at me, feeling there is probably a seed of truth in them.   1 2 3 4 5

Add up the circled numbers and place the total here: _____

If your total comes to less than 20, you probably are not paranoid.
If your total is between 21 and 40, there is a likelihood that you have
some paranoid tendencies. If your total is 41 or more, you probably are
a paranoid leader.

Do you see the traits of a paranoid leader in yourself? In what ways
does this type of leader mirror your dark side?

11

THE CODEPENDENT LEADER

As all too many children have, William Jefferson Blythe grew up in the home of an alcoholic parent. His childhood environment was characterized by instability and chaos. When he entered the world, Billy Blythe was already fatherless. Three months before he was born, his father was killed in an auto accident as he was traveling to pick up his pregnant wife and bring her to their new home in suburban Forest Park, Illinois. Not long after Billy's birth, without a husband to provide for her and her newborn son, his mother left him with his grandparents while she lived in New Orleans to pursue a degree in nursing in hopes of improving her chances of successfully raising her son. During her years of nurse's training, Billy was essentially separated from his mother until he was three years old. One of his earliest memories, Billy would say decades later, was "visiting his mother in New Orleans, then getting back on the train with Mammaw (his maternal grandmother) and looking out the window and seeing his mother on her knees, crying, as she waved good-bye."[1] It was a very traumatic experience for a young boy of one or two years old.

When Billy's mother, Virginia, returned home from her years in New Orleans she quickly and somewhat hastily married a man previously reported to be a wife-abuser by the name of Roger Clinton, who was also known for his heavy drinking, gambling, and philandering. In fact once, before they were married, Virginia caught Roger cheating on her but decided to marry him anyway, much to the displeasure of her family.[2] It was a dysfunctional marriage that was shaping a future president of the United States.

By the time he reached the first grade, Bill Clinton had already been exposed to significant family violence.

> One night Virginia dressed Billy up to take him to the hospital in Hope to visit her maternal grandmother, who was dying. Roger did not want them to leave. When she said she was going anyway, he hauled out a gun and fired a shot over her head into the wall. Virginia went across the street to the Taylors' and called the police. Billy slept at a neighbor's house.[3]

That episode was only the beginning. Young Bill spent many nights lying awake in bed listening to his parents' fights. The alcoholism of his stepfather and the violence it spawned continued to spiral out of control until Bill, then sixteen years of age, and his mother finally left Roger Clinton in 1962. The subsequent divorce proceedings were exceedingly difficult, and Bill Clinton was required to testify against his stepfather. As the family's oldest son, the years of chaos and violence had a profound emotional effect on the future president.

> The oldest son seemed emotionally distraught, not by the physical threats of his stepfather—he loomed over the man—but by the onus the family turmoil placed on him. He had come to understand that if the violence and abuse were to end, he

128

had to be the one to stop them. He was an adolescent put in the position of reversing roles so that, as he later said, "I was the father."[4]

Because of the turmoil and chaos within the family, a teenage Bill Clinton took responsibility to rescue his floundering family. He became the family hero. In the role of family hero Bill was excused from the family problems and "dispatched into the world to excel and return with praise and rewards that [would] make the entire unit feel worthy."[5] During his high school years Bill Clinton did not disappoint the family. He was an exceptional son and student.

In spite of Bill's success the Clinton household was constantly out of balance, frequently teetering on the very precipice of complete disaster. Bill, however, was determined to keep the family from experiencing an irreparable crash. His overachievement was a way of counterbalancing the irresponsibility and underachievement of his alcoholic father and of bringing stability to the home.

As with most dysfunctional families, the Clintons had become masters of denial. They learned to block out those episodes that might be the source of pain. The family also maintained a rigid set of rules, albeit silent and unwritten, that kept a lid on the family secrets. Speaking openly about the pain and chaos taking place inside the home would mar the illusion of civility they desperately hoped to project to friends and neighbors. As a result Bill was never given an outlet for the painful and confusing emotions he doubtless felt. In effect the family was forced to live a lie and deny any accusations of family abnormality. This denial is obvious when the president describes his childhood:

> Overall I was a pretty happy kid. I had a normal childhood. I had a good normal life. But at times it was really tough. I had to learn to live with the darker side of life at a fairly early period. But I wouldn't say it was a tormented childhood. I had a good life.[6]

One therapist assessed the president's childhood recollection as follows:

> This perception of self indicates Clinton's deeply ingrained denial of his youthful experience.... But one must grasp his deep-seated level of denial when he describes a childhood of repeated episodes of abandonment; parental alcoholism; marriage of his mother; divorce; remarriage; his stepfather's death; violence directed at his mother; his second stepfather's death; violence directed at his mother, brother, and himself; and gunshots discharged in his home as a normal life. A true description of Clinton's childhood would be: chaotic and highly abnormal.[7]

In his burgeoning role as family hero Bill Clinton developed a serious need to please others and make them happy. This need enabled him to acquire the ability to justify many otherwise questionable behaviors. He felt it was necessary to do this to keep the fractured family in balance.

All of these coping mechanisms so vital to his childhood became a deeply ingrained part of Bill Clinton's personality and behavior as an adult and later as our president. Bill Clinton is what has been labeled by the psychological community a co-dependent, and his codependency has had a powerful impact on his life and presidency. This behavior pattern has led to blatant lying regarding his extramarital affairs, draft record, and drug usage and has prompted the constant use of denial in an effort to defend himself against questions regarding these issues.[8] His need to please others led to what vice president Dan Quayle referred to during the 1992 presidential election as "shading the truth" and "doing a Clinton." Psychologist Paul Fick states that "Clinton's upbringing taught him to lie automatically, with no guilt, and to present excuses spontaneously. However, Clinton is no longer dealing with schoolhouse chums."[9]

As president, Bill Clinton flip-flopped on virtually every issue, saying what he thought certain interest groups wanted to hear at one moment, only to change his views later when faced with a group that held an opposing view. It is very likely that the president did not even recognize this as problematic behavior. It kept opposing factions placated. Yet these behaviors, produced by his troubled childhood, as well as others not dealt with here, crippled his leadership. Bill Clinton feared displeasing anyone, and this fear placed him in some untenable situations. In just the first two years of his presidency, he was accused of sexual misconduct, and he had to face the White House Travel Office scandal, the Whitewater affair, the tragic death of a close associate under questionable circumstances, and the dismissal of numerous high-level cabinet officers and staffers. All of these episodes were related in one way or another to the president's crippling codependency.[10]

Before his presidency was over, Bill Clinton was impeached by the House of Representatives for perjury related to testimony he gave before a federal grand jury about his relationship with Monica Lewinsky. Though the Senate ultimately voted not to uphold the impeachment and President Clinton completed his second term, the episode contributed to the increasingly partisan and destructive practice of politics in America. Even as we enter the election cycle for the 2008 presidential election, with Hillary Clinton running for the highest office in the land, the negative reverberations of that ugly episode continue to be felt.

Samson: A Man with a Need to Please

Samson grew up in an extremely restrictive environment with a secret he could not share with anyone—he could never get his hair cut. Because he was a Nazirite, Samson was subject to unusually strict rules of behavior; besides never cutting his hair, he was prohibited from drinking any fermented beverages, could not eat grapes in any form, had other specific dietary requirements, and was restricted from marrying outside of his people.[11] The Nazirite vow entailed a rigid, separatist lifestyle. Though the vow was ordinarily voluntary, done out of joy and a desire to be set apart for God alone, this was not exactly the case for Samson. It was prophesied to his parents that their son would be a Nazirite from birth (Judg. 13:5). Thus from the time he was born, he was expected to fulfill the vow of a Nazirite and violate it at his own risk. The reason for this separation to God was so that God could use Samson as his instrument of deliverance for Israel from the oppression of the Philistines. It was all a heavy load under which he had to live and an environment well-suited for the development of codependency.

Samson had a difficult time living up to these expectations from the very beginning. One of his earliest acts of rebellion was eating honey he found in the carcass of a dead animal, an act that made him unclean. He brought some of the honey to give his parents, who were also Nazirites, but neglected to tell them its source, possibly for fear of their response—a classic codependent behavior.

Samson's trouble in leadership was of his own making. He continually engaged in behavior that was self-destructive, another trait of the codependent. Though he knew he should not, he became involved with three different Philistine women, who plagued him and led him to his ultimate fall—the Timnite woman he took as a wife, the harlot at Gaza, and Delilah (Judg. 14:1–4; 16:1–20). One Bible commentator says:

> In spite of his [Samson's] great strength, he was not strong enough to control his own impulses. He was unable to withstand Delilah's seduction; and even when it became obvious that she was laying a trap for him, he still succumbed to her temptations and walked into it with open eyes.[12]

As stated earlier, any attempt to evaluate a Bible character's personality using contemporary definitions and diagnostics involves some conjecture. However, based on the behavior we are aware of in Scripture, it would seem safe to say that Samson was a leader who struggled with what we know today as codependency. Samson had a deep need to please others. It was very hard for him to disappoint anyone. In fact it was nearly impossible for him to say no even when saying yes was not in his best interest and ultimately was self-destructive. We also see in Samson a tendency to be a reactor, frequently reacting to the actions of the Philistines, such as his attempt at vengeance by burning the Philistine fields (Judg. 15:1–8). It is important for us to realize that even people divinely appointed and gifted by God, such as Samson, are not immune from the subtle inner workings of the dark side.

Keeping Peace and Easing Pain

The forces of codependency are powerful. Unlike the previous leadership types we have identified (compulsive, narcissistic, and paranoid), codependency does not fall into any one category of recognized personality disorder. Instead it is more of a generic trait or behavior that can be found in many different personality types and can be a component of many different personality disorders. There is not one widely accepted definition of codependency. Like the proverbial blind men and the elephant, the definition of codependency often takes shape from the person who is describing it. However, there is one definition that seems to be broad enough to encompass many different aspects of codependency:

> An emotional, psychological, and behavioral condition that develops as a result of an individual's prolonged exposure to, and practice of, a set of oppressive rules—rules that prevent the open expression of feeling as well as the direct discussion of personal and interpersonal problems.[13]

Though codependency is most often associated with people living with others who are compulsively dependent on something (e.g., alcohol, drugs, food, pornography, etc.), another important aspect of codependency is the social system that develops around these types of relationships. The codependent family adapts in different ways to counterbalance the socially unacceptable and embarrassing behavior of the dependent person. This often involves the development of strict rules—usually unspoken but clearly understood—that dictate how the family must behave and that govern how the codependent person is allowed to communicate in public. These coping behaviors call for covering up the behavior of the dependent person and restricting the codependent from giving full, honest expression to his or her true emotions or from discussing the problem with anyone else. This results in emotional repression that creates great stress for the codependent person.

It's interesting that the above definition has unique implications for those reared in very rigid, oppressive religious environments. Though there may be no unhealthy, compulsively dependent person in this environment, still those brought up in such homes experience many of the same dynamics. There are unspoken and unwritten rules governing what is acceptable to discuss and what is not. For example, admissions of unspiritual or "carnal" struggles (such as with lust, doubt, or fear) are not acceptable. Very strict religious groups hold their followers to very high, unrealistic standards that are impossible to consistently meet, resulting in a constant sense of failure and self-blame. Thus the members are unable to openly express their feelings or share personal problems with others and frequently develop codependent behaviors as a result.

Another aspect of codependency is the tendency to react rather than to initiate action. Codependents react to the behavior of the dependent person.[14] They react to the pain, problems, and behaviors of others in an effort to balance the family system, cover up the family problems, and maintain peace in their relationships.

Codependents take personal responsibility for the actions and emotions of others, often blaming themselves for others' inappropriate behavior, and they generally have a high tolerance for bizarre behavior in others. They will go to just about any length to avoid hurting a person's feelings even if it means they hurt themselves in the process. Avoiding confrontation at all costs, they often serve as peacemakers between hostile parties. Codependents appear to be extremely benevolent, always willing to take on another task, even to the point of being overextended, because saying no might hurt someone's feelings. As a result codependents become repositories of repressed anger and frustration. A typical scenario would involve someone's making a request of the codependent to take on a new project. Though the codependent does not want to take on the additional responsibility, he or she does, so as to avoid hurting the feelings of the person who made the request. Then, after accepting the new responsibility, the codependent may become angry and say, "I can't believe they would ask me; they know I am overloaded! What's wrong with them?" In reality, the simple solution to the codependent's problem would have been a polite but firm "no, thank you."

Codependents obsessively worry about the feelings of others, often to the point of becoming emotionally and physically ill. When they encounter an angry or upset person, their first response is to wonder what they may have done to make the person angry.

In essence the problem of codependency involves the ways that an individual copes with the behavior and expectations of those around him or her.

Codependent Spiritual Leaders

On one hand it is not difficult to see why codependents end up in positions of spiritual leadership. It is the ultimate venue for taking care of others. Unfortunately the person with severe codependency will experience great frustration in ministry. There are few professions where it is more difficult to maintain peace and please everyone than in ministry. Inevitably, the behavior of the spiritual leader that pleases some will alienate others.

A common manifestation among codependent spiritual leaders is their failure to confront and deal with inappropriate behaviors within the church. Even when a behavior is clearly unacceptable, the codependent leader can be terrified to address the situation for fear of hurting someone's feelings and risking the loss of approval that might come with such a confrontation. The natural result of such avoidance is the enabling of unhealthy and even unbiblical behaviors within the church.

Another negative aspect of codependency in spiritual leadership is that the codependent leader is often willing to take responsibility for the inappropriate attitudes and actions of others. When someone unceremoniously leaves the church with dissatisfaction, the codependent leader often feels responsible for the departing congregant's unhappiness and may attempt to placate the defector by smoothing over the "problem." This only allows the same thing to happen again in the future.

The codependent spiritual leader, particularly in the local church setting, can find his or her schedule out of control and the workload unbearable because the leader finds it nearly impossible to say no to the requests of church members. In an effort to keep everyone happy and gain approval, the codependent pastor can find himself being overtaken by the urgent needs of others while giving little attention to the overall direction of the church as a whole.

Ministry and Christian service organizations provide the perfect environment for a leader to focus on others to the exclusion of self. This often results in the codependent pastor or leader's failure to care for himself, producing burnout and other debilitating maladies.

Targeting Insights

- One manifestation of the dark side is the development of the codependent leader. Samson is one example found in the Bible.

- Some signs of a codependent leader include the following: Codependent leaders are peacemakers who cover up problems, rather than face them, in an effort to balance the group system. They may be very benevolent with a high tolerance for deviant behavior. Willing to take on more work so they do not have to tell anyone no, they react rather than act.

- At the heart of the codependent leader is a repressed and frustrated person who has trouble giving full, honest expression to emotions or problems.

Applying Insights

So how do you determine if you are codependent in the exercise of your leadership? Chances are that just reading the profiles in this chapter has brought you close to an answer. However, in an effort to provide more specific help, the following inventory is offered for your own personal assessment.

Read the following statements, circling the number that corresponds closest to your impressions about yourself.

1 = strongly disagree   2 = disagree   3 = uncertain   4 = agree   5 = strongly agree

1. I grew up in a family with one or more substance-dependent people (alcoholics, drug addicts, food addicts, etc.).   1 2 3 4 5

2. I grew up in a strict, legalistic religious environment that held its members to an unrealistic standard of behavior and discouraged open, honest communication about personal problems and struggles.   1 2 3 4 5

3. I am usually willing to put up with or ignore bizarre, embarrassing, or inappropriate behavior in others.   1 2 3 4 5

4. I often refrain from sharing my opinion in a group setting until I have heard the opinions of others in the group.   1 2 3 4 5

5. I frequently worry about hurting people's feelings by sharing my true feelings and thoughts.   1 2 3 4 5

6. I often feel responsible for problems I did not create.   1 2 3 4 5

137

7. I find it difficult to sleep because I worry about someone else's problems or behavior.   1   2   3   4   5

8. I find myself frequently overcommitted and feel my life is out of control.   1   2   3   4   5

9. I find it extremely difficult to say no to people even when I know that saying yes will result in difficulty for me or my family.   1   2   3   4   5

10. I constantly feel a sense of guilt but have difficulty identifying its source.   1   2   3   4   5

11. I feel like I never measure up to those around me and have self-deprecating thoughts.   1   2   3   4   5

12. When I receive compliments from others, I find it difficult to simply accept them without making qualifying statements.   1   2   3   4   5

Add up the circled numbers and place the total here: _____

If your total comes to less than 20, you probably are not codependent. If your total is between 21 and 40, there is a likelihood that you have *some* codependent tendencies. If your total is 41 or more, you probably are a codependent leader.

Do you see the traits of a codependent leader in yourself? In what ways does this type of leader mirror your dark side?

12

THE PASSIVE-AGGRESSIVE LEADER

He didn't want to go. In fact his aversion to the task impelled him actually to leave the country in hopes that the assignment would eventually be given to another spokesman. His assignment: Go to the enemy city of Nineveh and warn them of impending doom unless they change their ways and turn to God.

Jonah: An Angry Man

Because he walked away from the task God had assigned him, Jonah walked into a storm, the storm of God's discipline. As he attempted to escape God's call to Nineveh, his vessel of deliverance was swamped. Faced with the prospect of endangering the lives of others, Jonah confessed he was the cause of the storm, and, in response, the seamen threw Jonah overboard, hoping to save themselves. It wasn't until he was in the belly of the whale that Jonah finally expressed genuine sorrow for his reluctance to perform the task that God had called him to undertake (Jonah 2:8–9).

Jonah's sorrow and repentance would not last long. Once the storm spawned by his disobedience had passed, Jonah again developed a less than enthusiastic attitude toward the mission God reissued to him. To his credit, in spite of his reluctance and stubbornness, Jonah fulfilled the mission. One can only imagine Jonah lethargically preaching to the condemned Ninevites, intentionally trying to be ineffective in his proclamation, hoping the whole time that his efforts would be met with failure.

In spite of his less than stellar performance, God brought redemption and revival to the pagan city of Nineveh as a direct result of Jonah's preaching, but Jonah was not happy (Jonah 4:1). His anger produced a period of sulking and even caused him impulsively to cry out to God, "Now, O LORD, please take my life from me, for death is better to me than life" (Jonah 4:3). In the middle of Jonah's pouting and frustration, in a gracious gesture to shade him from the sun, God provided a plant for him to sit under, and "Jonah was extremely happy about the plant" (Jonah 4:6). The following day, when the plant withered, Jonah again became depressed and said, "Death is better to me than life" (Jonah 4:8). Jonah had a generally negative outlook on his life and the future.

In the life and ministry of Jonah we see a resistance to God's demand to perform an assigned task, bursts of sadness and anger, short-lived periods of contrition and sorrow for his actions, impulsive behavior, and a general negativity. Today Jonah would be classified as a passive-aggressive leader.

A Reluctance to Perform

Like Jonah the reluctant prophet, passive-aggressive leaders have a tendency to resist demands to adequately perform tasks.[1]

Their resistance is most often expressed through behaviors such as procrastination, dawdling, stubbornness, forgetfulness, and intentional inefficiency.[2]

This reluctance to perform stems from the fear of failure that comes when undertaking a significant project and from the fear that success may breed higher expectations, which could lead to some degree of failure in the future. What better way to avoid failure or the increased expectations that success may breed than by simply refusing to perform or intentionally performing inefficiently?

Passive-aggressive leaders are also prone to short outbursts expressing intense emotions, such as sadness, anger, and frustration. Most often their aggression lies just within the bounds of what is legal and socially acceptable and yet is still provocative. These outbursts are often followed by short-lived periods of sorrow and repentance.[3] All of this behavior demonstrates a certain impulsiveness.

Modern-day Jonahs are perennial complainers whose very presence demoralizes those whom they lead or with whom they interact.[4] Though they perform the tasks that are expected of them, it is with little or no enthusiasm, and they harbor anger and bitterness for being forced (so they think) to do so.

Because passive-aggressive people often are impulsive, their acquaintances and colleagues often feel edgy as they wait for the next outburst.[5] These leaders make people uncomfortable and often leave them feeling confused. Those who work with a passive-aggressive person often ask, "What did he mean by that outburst?" or "Where did that come from?" when the passive-aggressive launches into a tirade. Another tendency of these people is to exhibit impatience, irritability, and fidgeting when things are not going their way or when they become bored with the proceedings. Amazingly, God is able to use even passive-aggressive leaders to accomplish his purposes.

141

Passive-Aggressive Spiritual Leaders

Many passive-aggressive leaders in ministry find it difficult to set goals and implement plans for the future since these only provide the possibility for failure. Adding to this fear of potential failure is the passive-aggressive leader's pessimistic outlook, which causes him or her to say, "What's the use of planning or setting goals? Nothing is going to change around here anyway." They carry out their board's plans reluctantly. Standards and systems for measuring performance are resented and resisted by the passive-aggressive leader.

Leaders who are passive-aggressive may constantly complain about not having any support from their board and those they lead, citing that lack of support is one of the reasons why their effectiveness is impaired. Ironically, when others become involved with them and take a serious interest in helping them, these leaders quickly complain that they are not allowed to lead the way they want.

In board meetings and other settings, such as congregational meetings, the passive-aggressive leader may become impatient and irritable when things do not go his or her way. This frustration often results in an emotional outburst then or at some time in the future during a completely unrelated meeting.

It is not that these leaders are constantly angry or complaining. A majority of the time they appear to be happy, compliant, and satisfied with their job and organization. However, a pattern of erratic emotional behavior can be seen over a period of time. Because of this pattern passive-aggressive leaders are often the brunt of inner-circle jokes and comments such as "I wonder which pastor will show up for the meeting tonight?" or "I sure hope Pastor doesn't give us a performance tonight."

We remember a board member in a local church who demonstrated classic passive-aggressive behavior. As long as there was no agenda for change and no structured plans for the future, this board member was fine. The moment the pastoral staff and church board began moving aggressively and developing plans for the church's future he went into his passive-aggressive mode. At those meetings this board member would suddenly explode with an irrational, emotional outburst that would catch everyone by surprise. He didn't offer lucid arguments or better ideas; he simply began to rant and rave about broad generalities that remotely, if at all, touched on the issue at hand.

Well, as you might guess, these tactics were successful at halting progress time and time again. For years the ploys of this board member kept that church from implementing any plans that could have set a standard for success and moved the church to a new level of ministry and effectiveness. This is very often the way in which passive-aggressive leaders manifest themselves in spiritual leadership settings. Their rantings halt progress.

TARGETING INSIGHTS

- One manifestation of the dark side is the development of the passive-aggressive leader. Jonah is one example found in the Bible.
- Some signs of a passive-aggressive leader include the following: Passive-aggressive leaders are stubborn, forgetful, and intentionally inefficient. They tend to complain, resist demands, procrastinate, and dawdle as a means of controlling their environment and those around them. On occasion they will exert control through the use of short outbursts of sadness or anger.
- At the heart of the passive-aggressive leader are anger and bitterness as well as fear of success, since it will lead to higher expectations.

APPLYING INSIGHTS

Did the board member described in this chapter sound familiar? Have you ever responded as he did? How do you know if you are passive-

143

aggressive? The following inventory is intended to help you begin answering that question.

Read the following statements, circling the number that corresponds closest to your impressions about yourself.

1 = strongly disagree 2 = disagree 3 = uncertain 4 = agree 5 = strongly agree

1. I find myself resisting standards and procedures for formal review of my performance.	1 2 3 4 5
2. It is common for me to procrastinate on major projects that I must do.	1 2 3 4 5
3. I regularly resist others' ideas that could translate into increased performance or responsibilities for me.	1 2 3 4 5
4. I find myself constantly performing beneath my capabilities.	1 2 3 4 5
5. I experience periodic but regular outbursts of anger and frustration that are just within the bounds of what is considered acceptable behavior.	1 2 3 4 5
6. Occasionally I intentionally forget suggested projects.	1 2 3 4 5
7. Sometimes I give others the silent treatment as an expression of my anger.	1 2 3 4 5
8. I find myself telling others that nothing is bothering me when in reality I am seething inside.	1 2 3 4 5
9. I tend to be generally pessimistic and feel negative about my future.	1 2 3 4 5
10. Others have expressed to me that I make them feel uncomfortable.	1 2 3 4 5
11. Strategic planning and goal setting are difficult for me, and I resist such exercises.	1 2 3 4 5
12. Sometimes I catch myself trying to manipulate others in group settings by venting my anger and emotions when facing initiatives I do not support.	1 2 3 4 5

Add up the circled numbers and place the total here: _____

If your total comes to less than 20, you probably are not passive-aggressive. If your total is between 21 and 40, there is a likelihood that you have *some* passive-aggressive tendencies. If your total is 41 or more, you probably are a passive-aggressive leader.

Do you see the traits of a passive-aggressive leader in yourself? In what ways does this type of leader mirror your dark side?

144

As you likely have guessed, many leaders are a combination of the types just reviewed. In most leaders one or two types will have the strongest impact on the leadership style, while other types play minor roles. One way to see how they fit together in your own life is to plot the answers to the five inventories found in chapters 8 through 12. For each inventory take the number you entered as your total and divide by 5 (round off to the nearest whole number). Plot that number on the graph in figure 2 by starting at the center of the circle and moving toward the outside edge, counting the circles until you reach the total for that inventory. Place a dot on the circle representing your total. For example, if your total for an inventory is 40, you would place a dot on the eighth circle from the center (since 40 divided by 5 is 8). Once all totals for the inventories have been plotted, you can connect the dots with straight lines to see more clearly where the largest influence on your dark side is focused. This is the one(s) where the point is plotted farthest from the center. Figure 3 is done as an example.

So what will you do now with what you have learned about yourself? How can you use your newfound understanding to avoid a crippling leadership failure that humiliates you and

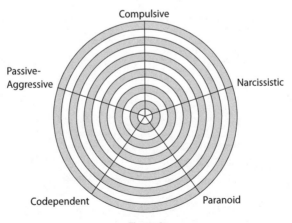

Figure 2

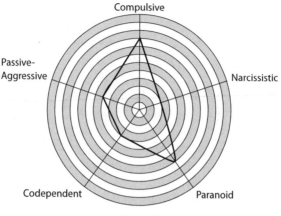

Figure 3

those you love? With increased awareness and understanding comes a greater responsibility to remove and overcome the dark side of your personality. It is now time to turn our attention to part 3 and the task of how we can begin to redeem our dark side regardless of the unique shape it has taken.

REDEEMING
OUR DARK SIDE

13

OVERCOMING THE
DARK SIDE

Though overcoming one's dark side is never an easy task, leaders are expected to exercise a higher degree of self-management, redeeming their dark side and thus mitigating its potentially negative influences. It is encouraging to know that leaders before us have been successful in doing just that.

Learning from Lincoln

Abraham Lincoln was a leader who safely guided the United States through one of its most difficult storms. His was an ominous leadership task: to hold together a fractured, warring nation until the issues dividing it could be resolved and unity restored. Like every leader, Abraham Lincoln was the product of his childhood experiences and traumas, which produced within him a dark side that compelled him to seek leadership and achieve success. His mother died when he was nine years old and a sister, Sarah, died when he was nineteen. After his mother's death, his father married a woman with three small children, forcing Abraham to live with several other people in a very small log cabin. Because he was an extremely awkward and unattractive boy, he was teased by his childhood peers, further developing his dark side.

Another profound influence on Abraham Lincoln's life was his father's lack of formal education and their failure to enjoy any intimate father-son relationship. As Lincoln began more aggressively to pursue the education his father never received, it led to an even greater estrangement between father and son. So deep was the rift between the two that later, when Lincoln received news that his father was on his deathbed, he refused to return home to say good-bye. He did not even attend his father's funeral.

As one might imagine, these were all major traumas. All of these childhood experiences, mingled with the future president's developing personality, created a powerful dark side. His early attempts to mask his dark side and achieve the approval of his peers took the form of telling funny stories and playing the comedian. As he grew older his dark side spawned within him the need to achieve success, resulting in many attempts to win public office. His sense of inferiority and lack of self-worth drove Abraham Lincoln to achieve a level of success and influence that would provide the salve for his painful childhood wounds.

Unlike many leaders Lincoln was painfully aware of his dark side and took proactive steps to prevent it from sabotaging his leadership. While he was able to capitalize on his numerous strengths, "he was also able to recognize his shortcomings, compensate for them, and play down his darker side."[1] Lincoln innately realized:

> All human beings have their weaknesses, but not all of us realize them, come to grips with them, or offset their negative impact. As a group whose primary endeavor is interacting with other

people, leaders *must* accomplish the paradoxical task of managing their darker sides.[2]

Armed with such self-knowledge, Lincoln was able to implement a strategy of personal management that enabled him to achieve greatness where many other leaders would have stumbled and fallen.

We may not be able to conclusively determine the depth of Lincoln's self-reflection and analysis of his childhood traumas, but we do know that he was acutely aware of his personal weaknesses and inner scars. When Lincoln was confronted with difficult leadership situations and when he became the target of cruel criticism that threatened to unmask his sense of inferiority and rekindle painful childhood memories and feelings, he didn't respond impulsively in an effort to protect himself. He knew that many of the feelings and negative emotions kindled by the difficult and threatening leadership experiences he encountered were the result of his own dark side. Consequently Lincoln was able to implement a series of self-management strategies that enabled him to soften his sharp edges and prevented him from responding in defensive, paranoid, or impulsive ways when he felt threatened. His self-management techniques allowed him to release inner pressure before it exploded into a significant leadership failure during a precarious period in United States history.

For example, Lincoln made it a practice never to display his anger in public. Instead he would express himself in a lengthy letter to the offending party. He would then hang on to the letter and read it periodically until the anger subsided, finally disposing of it, having never mailed it. It was in this way that he could vent his feelings without giving needless offense to others, which would create barriers to his leadership.

Lincoln was renowned for his witty comments and humorous anecdotes. Much as he did during his adolescent years, he used humor to defuse hurtful comments and personal criticisms before allowing them to stir his feelings of insecurity and inferiority. It was a practice that won the hearts and admiration of many political adversaries and critics in whom Lincoln's impulsive and defensive retorts could have created even greater hostility, hindering his ability to lead effectively.

Lincoln made conscious efforts to avoid conflict wherever possible. This desire to avoid conflict was not the result of codependent behavior, and it does not mean that Lincoln lived in a state of denial. Rather he realized that not every disagreement and issue was worth the energy required in conflict. Though there may have been a natural tendency for him to be controlling, he realized that controlling was not always necessary for a positive outcome and indeed was one of the symptoms of his dark side. As a result he was willing to allow his staff to handle matters in ways he often did not favor. On one occasion he stated, "Let minor differences, and personal preferences, if there be such, go to the winds."[3] On another occasion he lectured the assistant secretary of the navy about conflict:

> You have more of that feeling of personal resentment than I. . . . Perhaps I may have too little of it, but I never thought it paid. A man has not time to spend half his life in quarrels. If any man ceases to attack me, I never remember the past against him.[4]

The great majority of conflicts in leadership are the result of the leader's own sensibilities being offended, his ideas being rejected, his being outperformed by a staff member or not receiving the attention and respect he feels he deserves, and various other petty issues. These often become areas of conflict because they touch some raw nerve within the leader's dark side. They reinforce the leader's feelings of inadequacy, insecurity, paranoia, or some other feeling. Lincoln was aware of this and made it a practice to avoid conflict whenever possible by refusing to respond to those issues that were not crucial.

Do We Really Need to Overcome Our Dark Side?

The reality is we can never completely eradicate our dark side. It is always with us. Just as our shadow periodically disappears when the sun is absent, only to return later, we can subdue and overcome our dark side for significant periods of time but it is always with us.

For many leaders the journey to redeem their dark side must begin by recognizing the desperate need to do it. Warren Bennis, distinguished professor of business administration at the University of Southern California, has said that the experiences and events in our past "do not merely rule us, they inhibit us and make fools of us."[5] That is certainly true of the dark side when it is given free rein in the life of a leader. But what is it about our dark side that creates such urgency for us to overcome it as soon as possible? As we have seen throughout this book, the dark side has destroyed many leaders, churches, and families. Before we will ever have the incentive to overcome it, we need to understand the sobering results of failing to do so.

The truth is that we do not necessarily feel imperiled when we read of nationally known leaders who have fallen from grace because we find it difficult to identify with them. We most likely do not control budgets in the hundreds of millions of dollars, as they do. We do not influence tens of thousands of people when we preach or teach, as they do. Because we see our leadership and organization as having limited influence, it is easy to be duped into believing that the dark side is not a serious threat to us. But that is a lie. In fact it is a sign that our dark side is alive and well! We must be convinced that the dark side is a serious threat to how God wants to use us.

As we saw in part 2, each of us has a unique dark side as a result of our particular circumstances, personality, and experiences. Each manifestation of the dark side (compulsiveness, narcissism, paranoia, codependency, and passive-aggressiveness) has its own dangers. Whether we lead thousands each week or

153

just hundreds or whether we control a huge budget or a modest one, it would behoove us to overcome our dark side.

The Dangers of the Dark Side

A compulsive dark side allowed to operate unchecked can result in a personal and organizational rigidity that stifles creativity and frays our relationships with others. Compulsive leadership can produce a self-righteous, legalistic environment that alienates the people we are called to lead. Compulsive tendencies can result in workaholism or a painful emotional explosion and lead to complete burnout that may take years to recover from. Additionally the urge to control those we lead and live with more often than not results in alienation and rebellion as people react against our control. More than one marriage and church have been hopelessly fractured by such leadership.

If, however, like King Solomon and Jim Bakker our dark side takes the shape of narcissism, it can cause us to exploit those we have been called to lead. Rather than looking out for the needs of others, narcissism, if not overcome, will cause the leader to see people as so much "beef on the hoof," whose sole purpose is to feed the leader's insatiable appetite for bigger and better achievements. Narcissistic leaders literally have destroyed churches with building projects the churches didn't need and couldn't afford, again for no other purpose than to enable the insecure leaders to feel good about themselves temporarily. In the worst case rampant narcissism will even lead to unethical and illegal behavior as the leader is driven to achieve regardless of the price that must be paid.

Numerous spiritual Watergates have been perpetrated by paranoid leaders who lived in a constant state of denial. Acute distrust between pastors and boards, guerrilla-type church warfare, and an inability to enjoy genuine Christian fellowship are all the results of a leader's paranoid dark side run amuck.

Many codependent leaders have destroyed themselves in ministry as they tried in vain to keep an entire church happy and meet every other need while ignoring their own family and personal needs. Burnout, divorce, adulterous affairs, and physical illness can result when a leader fails to redeem his or her codependent behavior. It is highly likely that codependency has crippled more churches and Christian organizations than any other leadership malady.

Finally, there is the passive-aggressive leader who must live with the shame and consequences of his or her uncontrolled outbursts. Often, because of his or her erratic and strange behavior, the passive-aggressive pastor is forced to travel from church to church like an unwelcome itinerant preacher, never quite able to figure out why "those people" just don't love or want him or her.

This is but a cursory look at the troubles spiritual leaders may possibly avoid simply by learning to overcome their dark side. It seems that a little effort is worthwhile if it can prevent even some of these negative consequences and preempt a possible leadership washout. We must take responsibility to triumph over our dark side.

Redeeming the Dark Side

It is important to remember that though the term *dark side* may conjure up negative images, our dark side is not intrinsically evil. It is simply a part of being human. God can and does work through our dark side to accomplish his kingdom purposes and to elevate us to positions of leadership that we might not even have aspired to without the influence of our dark side. However, it is essential at some point that our dark side be redeemed to more adequately serve God's purposes and to be used less in satisfying our own needs.

It is God's desire that we soberly examine ourselves to learn about the things that are motivating us and the fears and anxieties that always accompany leadership. As we gain insight into these issues, we must give more and more of our unhealthy motivations and fears over to God. Failure to do so will almost always result in decreased effectiveness and the increased possibility of tragic failure.

We must realize that no amount of success or achievement will ever fill the holes created by our own unmet needs. Ultimately those needs can only be fully satisfied by a correct understanding and personal ownership of all that God has provided for us in his son, Jesus Christ.

Those with compulsive leadership tendencies must realize that God is sovereign and in total control of not only their life but also the circumstances that surround their life. God knows the beginning and the end. We can trust God with our life, even in its myriad of details.

The narcissistic leader must learn that no amount of achievement or personal recognition will slake his or her persistent inner thirst for a sense of personal adequacy and esteem apart from finding complete satisfaction in Christ.

Those who struggle with the traits of the paranoid leader need, like David, to trust that God is their protector and that he will be a fortress against all attacks on their leadership, whether real or imagined. The paranoid leader will need to learn that by promoting others God will see to it that the leader also receives his or her due.

Codependent leaders need to accept the fact that they are not responsible for the attitudes and actions of others and that pleasing God is more important than being liked by the people they serve. As leaders it is not our responsibility to "fix" everyone. We cannot always keep the peace and, in fact, at times should be the ones used by God to make people feel uncomfortable with their unacceptable behaviors.

Finally, the leader who struggles with passive-aggressive tendencies must learn that the motivation produced by a God-inspired vision and a well-crafted strategy to accomplish the vision is much more effective than the manipulation of emotional public outbursts.

It is through this process of learning about ourselves and progressively dealing with our dark side that we avoid its destructive paradox and allow God to exercise more control over our leadership. Eventually there will come a time when we can actually rest in our leadership as we calmly and confidently lead for God's glory rather than to satisfy ourselves.

Steps That Lead Out of Darkness

Obviously there is no quick and easy formula we can apply that will overcome the lifetime of experiences that have helped create our dark side. Walking out from under the shadow side of our personality will call for discipline and continual vigilance. It is a lifetime process, and *process* is the operative word here. Process indicates that there is a method or procedure that must be followed, a course to be taken. In chapter 14 I offer the organic process of composting as a metaphor for a spiritual process we can use in working through the steps offered in chapters 15–19.

This process and the accompanying steps are not offered as a simplistic formula for dealing with an exceedingly complex issue but rather as a basic framework on which we can continually build as we increase our understanding of the unique manifestations of our dark side and how it affects our lives and leadership. As was true in the lives of Abraham Lincoln and of Billy Graham, when we are outfitted with a proper understanding of our unique dark side, possess a willingness to honestly examine ourselves, and apply divine, spiritual truth, we can overcome our dark side and drastically minimize its negative effects in our life and leadership.

Targeting Insights

- The dark side of leadership can never be eliminated but can be overcome. Leaders can exercise a degree of self-management to keep their dark side in check.
- No simple formula can overcome a lifetime of experiences that have combined to form our dark side. However, as we apply God's truth to it, we can minimize its negative effects on our life, career, family, and ministry.
- Overcoming our dark side will take discipline, continued vigilance, and effort throughout our lifetime.

Applying Insights

What success have you had in the past over your dark side? Pinpoint your struggles and victories. To what degree are you willing to commit yourself to overcoming your dark side?

14

SPIRITUAL COMPOSTING

So now what are we to do with what we have learned thus far about our dark side? What is the process by which we can begin to deal with and overcome the negative traits we have identified? I (Sam) would like to suggest that a simple compost pile holds the secret to processing our dark side in a way that will bring about entirely new possibilities for our life and leadership.[1]

Spiritual Secrets from a Smelly Pile

In the far southwest corner of our rather large backyard, guarded by a slatted, wooden fence, lies the Rima family compost pile. For those unfamiliar with the idea of a compost pile in these days of trash compactors and garbage disposals, it is basically a rubbish heap, but not the type where one throws old tin cans, empty bottles, old bike tires, and airless basketballs. A compost pile is not just a fancy name for a mini garbage dump. It is the first stage in the process of rebirth for organic items no longer useful in their present state of existence—the place for garbage with a bright future.

During the spring, summer, and fall, the compost pile is the receptacle for our unusable organic refuse. After a good meal eaten with family in the cool of the evening, we take the leftover foodstuffs and place them on the compost pile. Things like watermelon rinds, corncobs, wilted lettuce, orange and grapefruit peels, chicken bones, and pieces of burnt meat all find their final resting place on the compost pile.

In addition to the inedible food, from spring through fall our grass clippings, fallen leaves, and weeds from the flowerbeds make their way to the confines of the compost pile. By the end of fall, our compost pile begins to put pressure on the fence that keeps it in place.

Yet when the last of the winter snow finally melts and the spring sun begins to warm the ground and coax the leaves from their buds, the once-large pile of unusable refuse has somehow shrunk to half or a third of its previous size. You see, that's the amazing and, yes, even miraculous nature of a compost pile. By putting all of our unusable organics in the same place and leaving them there for an extended period of time throughout the year, a very mystical process takes place. The chemicals provided by the various forms of refuse—catalyzed by the rain and sun beating down on them and the warmth that comes from a blanket of snow—create a reaction that begins to break down our household garbage and transform it into something from which life will spring forth.

By the time the spring thaw is complete and we can dig into the heart of the compost pile, it's not watermelon rinds and corncobs we find but rather humus, which can be tilled into gardens and flowerbeds to nurture new life. By a miracle of nature, our refuse has become rich, fertile humus.

The Process of Spiritual Composting

In a similar way, overcoming and redeeming our dark side requires that we engage in a process of spiritual composting. Judy Cannato, in her creative and insightful article "The Compost Pile," writes,

> The image of the compost pile articulates clearly the process of shadow integration, speaking to that deeper part of the self that understands what cannot be expressed in words. What the process of composting tells me is that there *are* parts of my personality that are not usable in their present form, but are nevertheless indispensable, because they provide the raw materials for personal growth. Composting also teaches me that I am responsible for participating in the process by identifying what is in need of transformation, by putting my refuse in a designated place, and then waiting as transformation occurs. Composting asks me to trust that I will eventually bear witness to what only God can do.[2]

Overcoming our dark side is not synonymous with running away from these less attractive aspects of our personality; it is a process not of somehow excising them from our life but rather of integrating them wholly into our life. As Cannato writes, these are parts of our personality that are not particularly useful in their *present* form. But that does not mean they are not useful at all; they just must be redeemed and transformed first. In fact, I am convinced that they hold the potential for our most effective ministry and leadership. Without them integrated into our life, our leadership will remain somewhat superficial and manufactured—a leadership of our own creation, built out of what we feel are our best qualities and greatest gifts.

But that was not what the apostle Paul relied on for the strength of his leadership: "On behalf of such a one I will boast, but on my own behalf I will not boast, except of my weaknesses" (2 Cor. 12:5 NRSV). Paul refers here to some sort of personal struggle or possibly a physical issue he had struggled with for an extended period of time. Some have speculated that it was poor

161

eyesight or depression. But whatever it was, it kept Paul from thinking too highly of himself and relying on his personal gifts and strengths for his leadership ability. In spite of pleading with the Lord to take this unknown ailment out of his life, the Lord said to him, "My grace is sufficient for you, for power is made perfect in weakness" (v. 9). And Paul responded to the Lord's decision to refuse his request by saying, "So, I will boast all the more gladly of my weaknesses, so that the power of Christ may dwell in me. Therefore I am content with weaknesses, insults, hardships, persecutions, and calamities for the sake of Christ; for whenever I am weak, then I am strong" (vv. 9–10 NRSV).

In a similar way, we need to be leaders who are willing to embrace our weaknesses—those presently unusable aspects of our personality—and to allow God, through the catalyst of the Holy Spirit working in and with us, to begin composting them into the spiritual humus from which our most powerful and fruitful ministry will come. Then, with Paul, we will give testament to the reality that the power of Christ is truly perfected in our weakness.

Creating Your Spiritual Compost Pile

The question still remains, however, as to how we are to participate in this spiritual composting process. What exactly is our role in the process? That is what the following chapters are about. They show how to take the necessary steps to identify those aspects of our life and personality that we perceive to be weaknesses and that are unusable in their present form, those aspects that we have tucked away in the shadow side of our personality out of public view. We will understand how they have developed over time and then learn how we can participate with God in composting them into something that will bring forth new life in and through us.

As you work through these chapters and do the suggested exercises, you will be creating your own spiritual compost pile.

And if you will keep it before you as you engage in your spiritual disciplines and spend time with God, giving your prayerful attention to those less desirable aspects of your personality under the catalytic guidance of the Holy Spirit, an amazing transformation will begin to take place. You will begin to witness what only God can do.

TARGETING INSIGHTS

- Engaging in the process of overcoming our dark side issues and allowing God to transform them is similar to the organic process of composting.
- Spiritual composting is about allowing the Holy Spirit to transform the less desirable aspects of our personality and then reintegrating them into our life, rather than denying them and trying to excise them from our life.
- Through spiritual composting, we can realize the truth of Paul's words in 2 Corinthians 12:9: the power of Christ is made perfect in our weaknesses.
- By practicing the discipline of spiritual composting, the Holy Spirit can transform our weaknesses into rich spiritual humus from which our most powerful and fruitful ministry will come.

APPLYING INSIGHTS

Take some time to consider what might prevent you from actively engaging in this process.

Begin a small compost pile at home and allow it to remind you of how God is at work, transforming your life through the process of spiritual composting. Actively participate with God in this process by using your journal to create your own spiritual compost pile (see pp. 202–4).

15

STEP 1:
ACKNOWLEDGE YOUR
DARK SIDE

The very week he graced the cover of *Time* magazine, heralded as the engineer of President Clinton's political resurgence in the face of seemingly insurmountable troubles, Dick Morris fell from his lofty position of public admiration. Surprisingly the man who was the central force behind the president's renewed emphasis on family values and conservative public morals found himself in a storm that swirled around allegations of his own acts of immorality and unethical behavior.

While Dick Morris was crafting public policy and campaign strategy, touting the importance of family values and hearty morals, he was spending the weekends with his wife in Connecticut and many of his weeknights with a two-hundred-dollar-an-hour prostitute in a posh Washington, DC, hotel just blocks from the White House. Morris also brashly shared political secrets with his love interest, on several occasions calling the

White House to speak with the president while allowing his lover to listen in on the conversation.

The scandal hit the airwaves the very week before the 1996 Democratic National Convention, when the president would triumphantly ride the wave of fresh public support generated by Dick Morris to a second nomination as president of the United States, a task deemed unlikely by many political pundits just months earlier. Morris's was an act of almost unbelievable proportions. What would possess a person who had worked so hard for the president's victory to behave in such a reckless and self-destructive way? How could a man of such apparent intelligence allow himself to be victimized by such behavior? The answer is quite simple: the dark side.

In the interviews and contrite discussions that followed his disastrous fall, Dick Morris acknowledged he had been victimized by his own dark side. More to the point, it was his denial and failure to acknowledge his dark side that led to his precipitous public tumble. He knew that what he was doing was wrong, yet he refused to acknowledge it and arrest the deviant behavior. According to an Associated Press interview, Morris acknowledged that he had become egotistical, arrogant, and out of control before his fall. He ignored his wife, his friends, and the rules, choosing instead to live in denial. "My sense of reality was just altered. I started out being excited about working for the President. Then I became arrogant, then I became grandiose, and then I became self-destructive."[1]

Dick Morris is simply another victim of the dark side, a victim who could have avoided such public and painful consequences had he simply acknowledged the existence of his dark side and taken the necessary steps to overcome an inner life that was reeling dangerously out of control.

Unfortunately, overcoming the dark side is not quite as simple as merely acknowledging that we have a shadow side to our personality. We must probe deeper to deal with the raw material that has gone into the making of our dark side (see chapter 4). As Christians we believe that it is our fallen human nature that is the primary culprit when it comes to the creation of our dark side and our ability to deny its existence. Therefore, our dark side needs not only to be acknowledged, it ultimately must be redeemed and restored. We must acknowledge our sinfulness and seek the forgiveness and redemption that can be found only through Jesus Christ. As we deal with this primal cause of the human dark side, the Holy Spirit of God will empower and direct us to overcome our dark side. However, even after taking these steps, we must be aware that we will be tempted to deny the periodic reemergence of our dark side. This is a battle we must constantly be prepared to fight.

The Danger of Denial

It is worthwhile to note that denying the dark side is not unique to twentieth-century politicians and leaders. Even King David, a man after God's own heart, fell victim to the dangerous consequences of failing to acknowledge the dark side.

The story is familiar. A powerful national leader of intelligence with rugged good looks is caught in the passionate allure of an associate's beautiful young wife. The divinely selected and ordained leader of God's own people is caught in the clutches of an adulterous affair resulting in the catastrophic consequences of a private scandal brought to public light.

King David's denial endured for more than a year until he was finally cornered by a persevering prophet who refused to be put off by a popular king's self-deception. There is no doubt that David was quite aware of his sin on that first evening with Bathsheba. But the rationalizations of the dark side proved to be a potent force with which to reckon. It was only after this grievous dalliance with his dark side that David acknowledged it and began taking the steps necessary to overcome it.

The good news is that we do not have to wait until we have experienced some irreversible leadership failure before we can begin redeeming our dark side. The time to begin is now! But every journey begins with that first step, no matter how insignificant it might seem.

Where the Journey Begins

Though it may sound simplistic, if we want to overcome our dark side, we need to start by acknowledging its existence and understanding the shape it has taken over the years. For many people who have spent a lifetime in church, this is not quite as easy as it sounds. All too often the Christian community, particularly evangelical Christianity, relegates the moral failures and other problems that result from the dark side of our personality to the realm of spiritual warfare and demonic attack.

Many Christian leaders have been taught to blame the "enemy" for their leadership failures. When a leader commits adultery, embezzles money from the church, or gets caught exposing himself, the most frequent explanation heard among the ranks of the faithful is "Boy, the devil is sure working overtime," with little attention given to the realities of human dysfunction. It is not that we are discounting spiritual warfare or demonic activity entirely when it comes to leadership failures. Clearly we face a menacing enemy who actively opposes God's people and work. But attributing all of our leadership failures and miscues to the devil or demonic influence lets us off the hook. When we do that, we transfer responsibility for our actions to a spiritual adversary we are evidently powerless to resist.

Instead of living in denial or rationalizing our dark side away, we need to recognize that the dark side of our personality is the result of normal human development—we all have one. It does not make us sick or bad, just normal. Like the rest of our corrupted humanity, our dark side can be redeemed with supernatural assistance.

Denial is a deadly disease from which every serious leader should be inoculated. Murder mystery writer Sue Grafton has made a career of studying the dark side of people to provide the foundation for her many novels. Speaking seriously in a recent issue of *USA Weekend* she submits, "We all need to look into the dark side of our nature—that's where the energy is, the passion. People are afraid of it because it holds pieces of us we're busy denying."[2] The sooner we stop denying our dark side's existence the sooner we will stop blaming the devil, our parents, bad breaks, and every other possible reason for our struggles. Blaming others is one of the symptoms that denial is taking place. It is always easier to deny we have any problem if we can lay the blame for our shortcomings at somebody else's feet.

There is nothing quite so difficult to battle as an invisible enemy that is a master of stealth, never seen or heard but devastating in its impact. Such is our dark side if we fail to take this first step of acknowledging and identifying it.

An Important Choice

When Sam's family decides to travel from Nebraska to his hometown of Spokane, Washington, the chosen route determines the nature of the journey. The journey can be made by traveling several different interstate systems. Two of those routes require more time, money, patience, and endurance. They require traversing major mountain ranges through seemingly endless miles of twisting roads. In contrast, the third route is a relatively straight shot. It carves at least a day off the journey, and with three young children constantly asking, "Are we there yet?" that is reason enough to take it. Before ever leaving Omaha, Sam's family must decide what kind of journey it will be—relaxing and enjoyable or taxing and tiring. It is difficult and costly to change routes in the middle of the trip. It is better for all involved to make the right choice before ever leaving the garage.

So it is on our journey toward God-glorifying leadership. We must make a choice. We can choose to acknowledge our dark side, practice a life of transparency before God, and let down our guard, knowing that he will begin his refining and empowering work in us; or we can choose to live in denial and even masquerade before God, fueling the ongoing development of our dark side. The course we choose determines the nature of our leadership journey and the condition in which we arrive at our final destination.

TARGETING INSIGHTS

- The first step toward overcoming your dark side is to admit that it exists and understand the shape it has taken in your life.
- Leaders usually deny the dark side and then blame their failures on others or circumstances rather than taking personal responsibility.
- To receive God's power over your dark side you must acknowledge its existence in your life and recognize God's empowering work through it (2 Cor. 12:9–10).

APPLYING INSIGHTS

1. Do you recognize the dark side in your own life?
   ___ Yes ___ No

2. What shape or form has the dark side taken in your life? Briefly describe it below as precisely as possible, noting how it appears privately and publicly in your life.

3. What are the past experiences that may have led to its development in your life?

170

4. How has it empowered your life and ministry in a positive manner?

5. In what ways has it eroded your leadership?

Take some time to reflect and pray, acknowledging your dark side and resting in God's ability to make you strong through it. Read prayerfully through 2 Corinthians 12:7–13.

16

STEP 2:
EXAMINE
THE PAST

Once we can admit that we do have a dark side that to some extent affects our exercise of leadership, we can begin in earnest to explore it. It is essential that such exploration begin with periods of serious and often painful reflection about our past. It is also vital that we avail ourselves of the probing, revealing ministry of the Holy Spirit, who can lead us into all truth, truth we would just as soon keep covered.

The Memories That Make Us

The leaders who have been driven to astounding levels of success and influence by painful childhood memories are too numerous to catalogue here. The point is that our past unavoidably impacts our present. Because some of our memories are painful, we have learned to push them into the recesses of our mind, hoping they will remain harmlessly locked away. In reality we are the sum of the experiences of our lives. The most successful and effective leaders recognize this and are able to separate fact from fiction in their childhood memories while understanding the role these memories have played in their personal development.

The purpose for examining the past is not for the assignment of blame, but for self-understanding. Though our reflections may lead us at some point to speak with people who played crucial roles in our development, casting blame is an absolutely fruitless and ultimately self-destructive practice.

We start by looking back to those childhood experiences that have impacted us in one way or another. "If you want to understand yourself and others, look into the areas of pain, sorrow, and rage," counsels Sue Grafton.[1] These events are not limited to such serious things as childhood physical abuse. Just because we were never abused does not mean we have not experienced other events that were traumatic to us at the time. We have all been touched by relatively harmless experiences that nonetheless have profoundly impacted us. Warren Bennis has said, "Given the pressures from our parents and the pressures from our peers, how does any one of us manage to emerge a sane—much less productive—adult?"[2] Every leader has run the gauntlet of embarrassing and humiliating childhood experiences that have left their indelible mark. These experiences are the very ones that must be explored and reflected on if we are to understand their full albeit subtle impact on our leadership. Often these experiences have created the missing blocks in our needs pyramid and are still driving us to achieve success as adults.

What Do We Look For?

So what past events do we look for? The events are many and often very innocent in nature. However, if they stand out in our memory, they are doubtless worthy of a closer examination. Events such as the divorce or death of our parents require thought. Rejections by peers or teenage love interests should be explored. The condition of our complexion during adolescence should not be ignored. Cruel statements by friends, the exact words of which we still painfully remember, must be probed. Academic failures, serious errors in judgment, humble family circumstances, and many other experiences all provide the fodder for our dark side and must be reflected on in an effort to understand how they may still be affecting us today as adults.

This process is not intended to be an exercise in morbid, microscopic introspection. It will not require hypnosis or any wacky therapy sessions to help us get in touch with our "primal child" or to utter cathartic screams of inner cleansing. Rather it is a simple process of remembering. It is looking back on our life and recalling those events that have shaped us and left their memorable mark. The things we can't remember are probably things that didn't impact us profoundly.[3] As we examine our past, it is vital to remember:

> We cannot change the circumstances of our childhood, much less improve them at this late date, but we can recall them honestly, reflect on them, understand them, and thereby overcome their influence on us. Withdrawal can be turned to hope, compulsion to will, inhibition to purpose, and inertia to competence through the exercise of memory and understanding.[4]

This, ultimately, is our goal. As we identify those experiences that were formative in our life, it is valuable to remember how we felt at the time of the experience. When other kids teased us unmercifully because of an acne problem, how did we feel? What were we thinking at the time? Did we silently fight back with *One of these days they won't be laughing. Someday my skin will be perfect; then we'll see who makes fun of me?* Is it possible we secretly pledged to ourselves that we would do whatever it took to become attractive and finally win the compliments of those very people who teased us? When we remember the rejection of peers, can we remember how inferior it made us feel and the promise we made to ourselves to do something great that would prove we were not inferior after all? The time our father refused to praise us for that report card containing all As and one B but instead reprimanded us for not getting all As, how did we feel? Did we at that time determine to earn our father's praise and approval no matter how long it would take? Such are the feelings that we need to get in touch with.

The reason it is important to recall not only the events but also the feelings they generated is that it is very often those same feelings that are still driving our behavior as leaders today. They have likely created some of the unmet needs in our life that we may be attempting to meet as adults through the exercise of our leadership. Warren Bennis says:

> Reflecting on experience is a means of having a Socratic dialogue with yourself, asking the right questions at the right times, in order to discover the truth of yourself and your life. What really happened? Why did it happen? What did it do to me? What did it mean to me? In this way, one locates and appropriates the knowledge one needs, or more precisely, recovers what one knew but had forgotten, and becomes, in Goethe's phrase, the hammer rather than the anvil.[5]

We must become the hammer that begins to shape our errant emotions and dark side rather than the anvil on which our dark side pounds us into its own distorted image. This can only take place as we become aware of some of those events that have created unmet needs never satisfactorily addressed. As we become aware of them, those events will be in the forefront of our mind. Once there, we can consistently examine how they may be driving us *before* they cause us to take a very wrong turn. After we have fully remembered and identified specific events and the feelings they generated, we can effectively deal with those issues and begin to disarm their powerful influence on our life and leadership.

Deal with the Past

As a result of your personal reflection it may become evident that you must talk with a person or correct some wrong. This may be necessary before you can ever feel released from the power of your dark side. If, for example, you discover that one of the childhood experiences that is driving you today is the failure to receive your father's approval, you may determine that it would be helpful to share how you feel with him in a nonthreatening way. Again, you are not blaming your father but letting him know of your personal discovery and then allowing him to respond in any way he feels is appropriate. You may want to say something like, "Dad, I've always wondered why I've felt such a need to succeed and impress others, even to the point of working too much. Just recently I've realized it's because I am really trying to impress you. I've always wanted to make sure you were pleased with me and that I wasn't letting you down in any way." By sharing with your father in this way, you have not blamed him. Instead, you have taken personal responsibility for this element of your dark side in a very concrete way. By expressing your feelings, you have taken away the power your father's lack of approval has had over your life. This type of encounter may need to take place with childhood friends, high school peers, parents, or others who were influential in your development over the years.

Another way that you may want to deal with your past is by writing letters expressing your recently discovered emotions. You may actually mail the letters to the parties concerned or you may never send them, simply using them as vehicles for processing your feelings about the present impact of past experiences. If you intend to mail the letters, it is vital that they be constructive, without placing blame.

177

Dealing with your past in an effort to gain freedom from the power of your dark side almost certainly will involve extending forgiveness in some form. Few things can control and cripple us in the present like unresolved conflicts and anger from the past. Neil Anderson in his bestselling book *Victory over the Darkness* has noted:

> Forgiveness is necessary to avoid entrapment by Satan. I have discovered in my counseling that unforgiveness is the number one avenue Satan uses to gain entrance to believers' lives. Paul encouraged mutual forgiveness "in order that no advantage be taken of us by Satan; for we are not ignorant of his schemes" (2 Cor. 2:11). Unforgiveness is an open invitation to Satan's bondage in our lives.[6]

Obviously these same effects will also impair your ability to provide balanced, Christ-centered leadership. Because God has forgiven us in Christ, we are required to deal with others in the same way: extending mercy rather than seeking revenge, and forgiving rather than holding a grudge. This can be especially difficult when the offending party has not yet recognized the hurt he or she has caused or refuses to admit to ever doing anything that requires forgiveness. But as followers of Jesus Christ, we have been told, "If you forgive others for their transgressions, your heavenly Father will also forgive you. But if you do not forgive others, then your Father will not forgive your transgressions" (Matt. 6:14–15).

Your exercise of forgiveness may involve forgiving others for the way they treated you. You may also need to forgive yourself for mistakes and failures that still haunt and control you. Regardless of the issues involved, unforgiveness is one of those things that must be dealt with before you can ever move ahead unencumbered. This forgiveness can be extended via letter or personal contact; the mode is not nearly as important as the fact that you do it.

As an aid to taking this step of forgiving and dealing with the past, we highly recommend the "Twelve Steps to Forgiveness" in Neil Anderson's *Victory over the Darkness*.[7] These practical steps will help put skin on the ethereal concept of forgiveness and enable you to move beyond the issues and conflicts of the past that may be crippling you in the present.

TARGETING INSIGHTS

- The second step toward overcoming your dark side is to examine your past. It is crucial that you avail yourself of the work of the Holy Spirit to lead you into all truth.
- You should begin by recalling the events that have shaped your life and left an indelible mark. As you remember, you must identify the feelings generated within yourself that are still motivating you as a leader today.
- Gaining freedom from the power of your dark side involves extending forgiveness in some form. Your exercise of forgiveness certainly will involve others but includes forgiving yourself.

APPLYING INSIGHTS

1. What events from your past still come to mind after all these years? Briefly list them below.

2. Describe in one- or two-word statements how you felt or feel about each incident.

3. Reflect on each of the memories listed by answering the following questions.
   - What really happened?

   - Why did it happen?

179

- What did it do to me?

- What did it mean to me at the time?

- What unmet need did it leave in my life?

- How has this experience surfaced in my adult life?

- Where do I see it in my life today?

4. Based on your rethinking of each past experience, what is God leading you to do today?
   - Is there someone you need to talk to?

   - Is there a letter you need to write?

   - Is there a phone call you need to make?

   - Is there a person, group, or organization you need to forgive?

   - Is there a prayer you need to offer to God?

5. What will you do? See Matthew 6:14–15.

17

STEP 3:
RESIST THE POISON
OF EXPECTATIONS

The steps of acknowledging our dark side and engaging in personal reflection involve issues that have their source within us. They are steps that we can take in an effort to deal with emotions and behaviors that to some degree are self-generated and self-imposed. This third step, in contrast, requires us to confront expectations imposed upon us by others.

The Fear of Disappointing Others

On arriving in Scotland, the American minister and two of his church's board members were anxious to meet their counterparts at a mission work they had been commissioned to visit. Coming as they were from a strong evangelical church in the States with a rich heritage in missions, the men were anxious to see what exciting things were being accomplished through the ministry of this church they were supporting. As they left their airport shuttle at the curb, they climbed the centuries-old stone stairs that led to the rectory. Before they could knock to announce their presence, the resident pastor flung open the door and with his arms fully extended in a grand gesture befitting a eucharistic blessing, he enveloped the visitors in a warm embrace. *Ah, the warmth of Christian fellowship extends even across the Atlantic,* thought the Yanks.

After appropriate hugs and greetings the Scottish pastor ushered his guests into the wood-paneled comfort of the study and directed them toward ancient leather wingback chairs. It was an exciting occasion, one that called for a proper inauguration. The host reached for a richly grained wooden box that smelled of cedar. When he opened it, his guests saw a treasured store of choice cigars. With obvious pride he offered each guest a cigar. The two laymen nervously looked at one another, then gazed toward their own pastor, not quite sure of the proper protocol at such an awkward ceremony. With sullen faces belying more than a little disapproval, both laymen refused the offer. Their pastor, however, eagerly snared a cigar from the humidor and lit it up, appreciatively admiring the curl of thick smoke that rose to the beamed ceiling. The Scottish rector smiled with satisfaction.

Next the Scot went to his credenza and collected from it four small glasses and an etched-glass decanter containing a caramel-brown liquid. The laymen looked nauseous. Surely this was the reason that Christianity had died in the British empire! When they returned home, they would see to it that the church reconsidered its financial support for such a carnal operation. They refused the brandy with even less decorum than they had rejected the cigars. Their host was by now looking worried, wondering if he had somehow done something wrong. The American pastor, to the chagrin of his traveling companions, once again accepted the offering and took a satisfying sip. After an hour of visiting, confirmation of the coming itinerary, and a departing benediction, the Americans left. Once in their cab the laymen wasted no time before launching into an interrogation of their pastor. "Pastor, how could you!" exclaimed one of the board members. "I can't believe you did that!" vented the other. "I thought we were here to support their ministry and encourage them in their evangelistic efforts—it's no wonder the church is dead over here!" After a moment of silence the pastor replied with more than a hint of disgust, "One of us had to act like a Christian."

Acting Like Christians

What does it mean to act like a Christian? What are the legitimate, biblical expectations that can be placed on spiritual leaders? Today many rank-and-file evangelicals would pronounce the behavior of the pastor in our apocryphal story highly suspect. While his actions may have been more consistent with the example of Christ and his heart and motives more in tune with the Savior's, on the basis of two external behaviors clearly not legislated against in Scripture, he would be judged as carnal at worst or the possessor of questionable judgment at best. Such a pastor would be in immediate danger of lost respect and credibility. In fact we suspect that any evangelical pastor today who participated in a wedding party where alcohol was served as Jesus did at Cana would quickly be accused of condoning sinful behavior, never mind what would be said if the pastor ran to the store to buy more wine when the family's supply ran low.

In today's evangelical subculture it seems that the answer to the question, What does it mean to act like a Christian? is increasingly at odds with the teaching of Scripture. From both within and without, Christian leaders are faced with a confusing and expansive menu of expectations when it comes to being a spiritual leader. Everything seems to be dictated, from where they should live to what they should do for entertainment. Many of these expectations are internally generated by leaders themselves, while others have been created and placed on them by those they lead. Like the liturgists and mainline denominations that we readily accuse of being overly burdened by human traditions, we have developed our own expectations and spiritual standards of measure not entirely supported by the Scripture we hold so high. Our legalism is well-intended; nevertheless it is also quite repressive and destructive for those who must live and lead under its weight. For too many Christian leaders, the Reformation's liberating cry of *"sola scriptura"* has been forgotten. Like the Galatians of old, we may be guilty of trying to attain our holiness through human effort and regulations rather than through the sanctifying work of the Holy Spirit within us. Where do these extrabiblical expectations we labor under come from? Why do they seem to have such a powerful, even destructive, influence over our behavior? These are some of the issues we must deal with in our efforts to overcome the dark side.

The Power and Pain of Expectations

Expectations. What exactly are they? The word itself is obviously derived from the root word *expect*, which in its simplest form means to consider something reasonable, due, or even necessary. However, the word can also mean to be obligated or bound by duty. When we have expectations of a product, such as a vacuum cleaner, we expect that it will perform in a reasonable manner and fulfill the necessary tasks for which we have purchased it. When a vacuum fails to consistently remove dirt from our carpet, we are dissatisfied with the product because our expectations have not been adequately met. This would seem to be a legitimate arena for the expression of expectations.

In a similar way, we can have expectations of people. For example, we expect our children to behave in school. We do not expect them to be models of perfect behavior, free from all antics appropriate to their age; that would be unnatural. Neither do we expect them to earn straight As at every report; that would be unrealistic. However, we do expect them to demonstrate respect for their teachers and obey the instructions they give. We do expect them to complete their assignments to the best of their ability and put forth honest effort. These are reasonable expectations.

Though expectations are necessary to a degree, they can also be a two-edged sword in our lives. On the one hand, we should have healthy expectations of our children, spouses, and leaders. Such expectations communicate that we have confidence in them and believe that they are capable of achieving a certain standard of behavior or accomplishment. These healthy expectations can motivate the people toward whom they are directed to behave and achieve beyond their current level. On the other hand, when our expectations become unrealistic or are selfishly motivated, they can become very destructive in the life of the person toward whom they are directed. When a parent expects a child to be the valedictorian of the high school class, this expectation places an incredibly heavy burden on the child. When a husband expects his wife to maintain her teenage figure or look like one of the sleek, skeletal supermodels the media holds up as the standard for female beauty, his expectations can have very negative effects.

You see, expectations can either propel people to achieve or they can produce pain and failure. The same is true when it comes to the expectations we place on ourselves as leaders and the expectations we allow others to place on us. Very often the expectations—spoken or unspoken—placed on us by others serve as the driving force behind our achievement and aspirations to succeed. Many leaders have attained high levels of success because of the expectations of others. In fact there have been many leaders, like the Spanish dictator Francisco Franco, who have been motivated to achieve extraordinary levels of success precisely because others expected them to fail. Whether positive or negative, whether self-imposed or imposed on us by others, expectations can powerfully influence our lives. Unfortunately they can also be very destructive.

Expectations That Destroy

During the 1980s a young quarterback by the name of Todd Marinovich was taking the football world by storm. Todd was the quarterback for the University of Southern California Trojans and was a model of what the position was all about.

From the time Todd was an infant his father, Marv, had planned for him to be a quarterback at USC, his own alma mater. With that goal in mind Marv placed a football in Todd's crib before he could even speak. Todd's father kept him on a regimented diet free from all food additives. Nothing but wheat germ and fresh fruit was good enough for a future pro quarterback. When young Todd attended the birthday party of a friend, he was not allowed to enjoy birthday cake with the other children. Instead he ate the healthy snacks his father had packed for him. As a teenager there were no Big Macs or Whoppers for Todd, no milk shakes or Snickers allowed. He was going to be a star and there was a price to pay. From his earliest days Todd worked with a professional trainer to help sculpt his scrawny body into an image of athletic beauty. There was another trainer who fine-tuned his throwing motion and continued to refine it with hours of practice, all under the expectant eye of his father.

By the time Todd made it to USC, he was the talk of the football world. As a freshman he was already being touted as a potential Heisman Trophy candidate and as the next Bart Starr or Johnny Unitas. But an unexpected thing happened to Todd on the way to the pros. By his junior year at USC he began having difficulty controlling his behavior. He frequently disagreed with his coach. While Marv Marinovich continued to manage his boy's career, the boy was beginning to reel dangerously out of control. It wasn't long before Todd was skipping practices and jeopardizing his entire team's prospects for success. He began experimenting with drugs and allowed his formerly neat crew cut to cascade to his shoulders in brilliant red locks. After just two years at USC Todd Marinovich, the blue-chip quarterback, groomed by a doting father for a future trip to the Pro Football Hall of Fame, was on a collision course with the dark side.

In an attempt to salvage some of the steam from Todd's rapidly evaporating career, his father orchestrated a move that had him drop out of USC and sign a contract with the Los Angeles Raiders, long known for their renegade players. In Marv's mind Todd was simply too advanced for college football. Perhaps he was being held back by a limiting system that failed to recognize the extraordinary gifts of a prodigy. But Todd couldn't make it with the Raiders either. He opted instead for the career of a beach artist, enjoying for the first time an unshackled existence free from the rules and expectations that were squeezing the life out of him.

Todd Marinovich is an example of the destructive power of expectations gone berserk. The bar had been set so high for Todd there was no way he could maintain the level of performance necessary to jump it. His response to the pressure? Run in the opposite direction and break every rule.

Whether they are young sports prodigies like Todd Marinovich and fallen tennis star Jennifer Capriati, entertainers like movie star Macaulay Culkin, or ministers and other Christian leaders, the weight of expectations can cause even the most compliant and well-intentioned person to snap under the heavy load.

Not Just Football Fathers

How sad it is that a young man with so much potential could be driven to the point of despair and reckless rebellion by something as seemingly benign as expectations. Yet we are seeing the same dynamic with increasing frequency within the ranks of spiritual leadership as well. There are too many young men and women entering the ranks of spiritual leadership today carrying the heavy load of unrealistic expectations.

During their seminary careers these young leaders have been exposed to the awesome success of churches like Willow Creek Community Church, Saddleback Valley Community Church, the Crystal Cathedral, and other rapidly growing megachurches of lesser renown, and the unspoken expectation is that they too will achieve equal success. They are briefed in the latest marketing techniques and methodologies that promise an opening-day attendance in the hundreds and they begin making plans to provide leadership for an instant church of two hundred. Church planters leave the ivy-covered halls of seminary ready to build the next megachurch that they feel certain will be the subject of a Peter Jennings special report or a glowing profile in an issue of *Christianity Today*. They are completely unprepared for the realities of life in the church-planting trenches. Then when success doesn't come as quickly and as grandly as they expect, when their expectations are slammed against the wall of reality, the gulf between their expectations and reality becomes a ministry-shattering crisis.

The same is true for other spiritual leaders as well. Whether it is a Christian counselor with expectations to build the next Minirth-Meier Clinic, the administrator of a Christian university who is expected to take his school to the same level as a Wheaton College, the young evangelist expected to replace the aging Billy Graham, or the leader of a nonprofit organization planning to change the world, expectations can set leaders up for a tremendous fall.

Most often these disappointments are fueled by a dangerous combination of both internal and external expectations. Many of those who aspire to positions of leadership, particularly high-profile leadership, carry with them their own latent expectations that have been created by their dark side. They have set a high standard for themselves. They are often their own worst critics. So when their expectations for whirlwind success and national recognition are mingled with the expectations of a denomination or board, the resulting elixir can be quite toxic. Under its influence many leaders have found their way into the arms of a secret lover in a desperate attempt at personal validation. Others have resorted to the use of pornography or other self-destructive behaviors as a way to escape the pressure of the expectations they have failed to meet.

Unrealistic expectations are intensified because of their cumulative effect.

> The expectations placed on a pastor and his family by themselves and by others combine to make a cumulative list of musts that is often unbiblical and unreasonable. This is because the expectations are both numerous and contradictory.
>
> Every person in a given congregation comes to the church with differing backgrounds. Some are old. Some are young. Some come from rural churches where they were involved in almost every facet of their church's life. Others come from large suburban churches where there was a program for everything. Some come from no church background and therefore don't know what to expect. (Bless them.) The pastor has his own background and his own heroes. All this means that there are a hundred or more different lists of expectations of the pastor. Sooner or later, the pastor finds out about all of them. Since his professional well-being rests on the good will of the people he serves, he does his best to meet this cumulative list of expectations.[1]

Pastors and other leaders have always faced unrealistic expectations. The difficulty today is that each individual has his or her own set of expectations; few are commonly agreed on. Thus the intensity of expectations is multiplied, creating a burden rarely experienced in days gone by. In 1995 Dr. Robert Edmondson surveyed and interviewed thirty pastors who had left pastoral ministry permanently and thirty churches that had lost their pastors. Dr. Edmondson found that the second leading

189

reason pastors left the ministry was the unwritten expectations of the pastor (the first was "burnout").[2]

Because the influence of expectations is so powerful, many leaders often live life at a dangerously frenetic pace in an effort to meet all of them and satisfy all of the people who have made them known. Unfortunately this is often self-defeating. The harder they work to satisfy all expectations, the greater the number of expectations that are placed on them. They create for themselves a reputation as the person to go to when there is a big project that needs to be done right. As a result, instead of quieting the crescendo of expectations around them, their frantic and successful efforts actually work to increase expectations. It becomes a vicious cycle. This pace cannot be maintained indefinitely. After a prolonged period of such frantic living, the leader's internal engine shuts down, and he or she comes to a grinding halt.

Every Engine Needs Oil

As a twelve-year-old, Sam was the proud owner of a go-cart powered by a little two-cycle lawn mower engine. He was the most popular kid on his block. Before giving him the green flag on the local elementary school playground, Sam's father explained how important it was to check the oil in the engine each time it was filled with gas. Because the little engine on that go-cart had to work extra hard, failing to keep it well oiled could result in the pistons freezing up in their cylinders. One day Sam was burning around the playground at speeds topping fifteen miles per hour, weaving in and out of tetherball poles like Danny Sullivan on a Formula One track, the wind blowing through his hair, the little Briggs and Stratton musically singing, when without warning the engine stopped, spinning him out of control. He had failed to check the oil. The joy of owning a go-cart was over. The go-cart engine could only run so long without oil—then it just shut down.

The same principle applies to leaders. Every leader needs to keep his or her engine well lubricated to perform at optimum efficiency. We can run at a frantic pace, driven by the expectations of others and ourselves, for only so long before we freeze up and spin dangerously out of control.

Burning the Engine

At twenty-eight Janet is a successful young Christian businesswoman, serving as a midlevel manager for an international corporation. She has risen within her company quickly and is expected to contend for a vice president position before long. She is married and the mother of two girls and one boy. She and her husband are both active in their church, and Janet serves in several leadership positions. She is an influential person who is respected by those she works with and has a reputation for getting the job done with excellence. On the outside Janet is a picture of composure and organization, the envy of many who know her.

However, all is not well in Janet's life. She labors under an almost unbearable load of expectations she has placed on herself as well as the expectations she feels from her parents, husband, friends, and fellow church leaders. Janet feels she is expected to be the perfect mother to her children and loving wife to her husband. Her parents expect her to be a dutiful daughter who will reflect well on the family name, and God expects her to be a faithful church leader. At the same time she feels the expectations of friends to maintain the close relationships they enjoyed in college. Because Janet fears disappointing anyone, she lives her life at a breakneck pace, trying to keep numerous balls in the air at the same time. Unfortunately the better she is able to do this and maintain her outward appearance of composure, the more balls she finds thrown at her. To drop a ball is not an option for Janet.

Recently Janet's husband has grown concerned. Janet has been keeping some strange hours and engaging in uncharacteristic behavior. In recent months she has often joined her younger, single friends after work for a drink at a local club frequented by many young professionals. Though that in itself is not wrong or sinful, the problem is that she has been staying out until 1:00 or 2:00 in the morning without letting her husband know where she is or when she will be home. Rather than spending what little discretionary time she has at home with her family, she has opted to spend it with casual friends who are not married, do not have families, and do not share her Christian perspective.

These excursions with her friends and the innocent rebellion against her structured life are Janet's way of letting off steam. It is her way of balancing out the expectations she lives under and finding a measure of relief from their back-breaking weight. Janet is aware of the destructive dynamic at work in her life and will begin dealing with the issues that have created it before it's too late.

Too Late for Some

There are spiritual leaders too numerous to mention, many of them pastors, who are engaged in the same battle as Janet. In their attempts to live up to their own expectations and those they perceive from parishioners, denominational leaders, God, parents, and just about everyone else, they are living close to the red line, the edge. They sense an expectation to be perfect: no R-rated movies of any kind—someone might find out; no glass of wine with a nice dinner—the rumor mill would get wind; forget certain kinds of music—a parishioner might think him or her carnal; a dance with the spouse is out of the question; certain television shows are *ipso facto* off-limits; driving foreign-made cars would burst someone's bubble; and living in a particular neighborhood would invite questions as to the minister's sincerity and commitment to service. Add to these prohibitions the normal expectations placed on pastors—attend all services, visit all sick people, be available at all hours. The pressure becomes unbearable.

The suffocating list of extrabiblical expectations goes on and on. Sooner or later these leaders must come up for air. After living in this repressed condition for a prolonged period of time, it is not uncommon to find these leaders (who would never dream of watching an R-rated movie or touching a drop of alcohol) engaged in an extramarital affair. Such was the case with Jimmy Swaggart. After years of preaching a legalistic standard of holiness based on human performance and the necessity of avoiding every form of "carnality," his explosion came in a hotel room where he was found with a known prostitute. The steam produced by such pressure-cooker living will always seek to escape; and if it cannot it will cause an explosion.

Like a go-cart, these leaders desperately need something that will reduce the friction and pressure in life created by unrealistic expectations. Where can we find this protecting and liberating oil? What can we do to reduce the friction and pressure created by unrealistic expectations, whether we have placed them on ourselves or allowed them to be placed on us by others? Let us suggest some oil that will enable our engines to begin running smoothly again. This oil can restore the joy and freedom to the exercise of our leadership.

The Oil of Grace

More than anything else, a proper understanding and personal application of the grace of God can liberate us from the poison and pressure of unrealistic expectations. If anyone understood the pressure of unrealistic expectations, it was Jesus. He entered a leadership environment where expectations were the order of the day. The Pharisees had developed expectations of the lives of others into a special art form. Jesus characterized the Pharisees as people who would tie up heavy burdens, and lay them on men's shoulders; but they themselves are unwilling to move them with so much as a finger . . . they do all their deeds to be noticed by men; for they broaden their phylacteries and lengthen the tassels of their garments.

Matthew 23:4–5

The Pharisees were legalists who would "strain out a gnat and swallow a camel" (Matt. 23:24). They were leaders who, because of their rigid, legalistic standards, outwardly appeared righteous but inwardly were full of hypocrisy and lawlessness (Matt. 23:28). They were quick to lay their expectations not only on the people they led, but also on fellow leaders like Jesus. They demanded that he meet their expectations. Jesus refused to accept the expectations of others. He shattered them all. Because he did not fit their mold he was labeled "a gluttonous man and a drunkard, a friend of tax collecters and sinners!" (Matt. 11:19). In spite of the labels, Jesus insisted on living in grace, accountable to his heavenly Father and faithful to the mission for which he had been sent.

To those who labored under the heavy load of expectations placed on them by the Pharisees and the oppressive religious establishment Jesus said:

Come to Me, all who are weary and heavy-laden, and I will give you rest. Take My yoke upon you, and learn from Me, for I am gentle and humble in heart; and you will find rest for your souls. For My yoke is easy, and My burden is light.

Matthew 11:28–30

Throughout the Scripture we are encouraged to live lives of freedom, not legalism, fully enjoying the grace of God:

If the Son makes you free, you will be free indeed.

John 8:36

194

Therefore no one is to act as your judge in regard to food or drink or in respect to a festival or a new moon or a Sabbath day—things which are a mere shadow of what is to come; but the substance belongs to Christ. Let no one keep defrauding you of your prize [the freedom provided by God's grace] by delighting in self-abasement. . . . If you have died with Christ to the elementary principles of the world, why, as if you were living in the world, do you submit yourself to decrees, such as, "Do not handle, do not taste, do not touch!" . . . These are matters which have, to be sure, the *appearance* of wisdom in self-made religion and self-abasement and severe treatment of the body, but are of no value against fleshly indulgence.

Colossians 2:16–23 (emphasis ours)

It was for freedom that Christ set us free; therefore keep standing firm and do not be subject again to a yoke of slavery.

Galatians 5:1

For the law of the Spirit of life in Christ Jesus has set you free.

Romans 8:2

And you will know the truth and the truth will make you free.

John 8:32

Obviously there is a corresponding responsibility that comes with God's grace and freedom. We are not to exercise our freedom at the expense of another believer's spiritual well-being. We are not to use our liberty as a license to engage in unrestrained freedom that leads to sin. As Paul says, "You were called to freedom, brethren; only do not turn your freedom into an opportunity for the flesh, but through love serve one another" (Gal. 5:13).

However, as long as we do not allow our exercise of freedom to lead to the violation of express scriptural prohibitions and principles or to cause the destructive offense of an immature

195

believer, we are free to enjoy what God has provided. Paul reaffirms this principle:

> The one who eats is not to regard with contempt the one who does not eat, and the one who does not eat is not to judge the one who eats, for God has accepted him. Who are you to judge the servant of another? To his own master he stands or falls; and he will stand, for the Lord is able to make him stand.
>
> Romans 14:3–4

Rather than allowing others to dictate our behavior before God, we would be much wiser and healthier if we followed Paul's admonition to follow our own conscience under the guidance of the Holy Spirit. "The faith which you have, have as your own conviction before God. Happy is he who does not condemn himself in what he approves" (Rom. 14:22). We need to realize that legalism is always a human attempt to legislate holiness and usurp the restraining, controlling work of the Holy Spirit in a believer's life. Requiring others to live by legalistic expectations says that we do not believe the Holy Spirit of God is able to get the job done.

Charles Swindoll, the prolific author who also serves as the president of Dallas Theological Seminary, has stated, "If anybody needs to breathe free, to join The Grace Awakening, those in vocational Christian service do!" He continues, "I can tell you without hesitation that one of my major goals for the rest of my years in ministry is to provide more and more breathing holes for fellow ministers who have lost the joy of freedom, who know little of the charm of grace."[3]

If we are to overcome the power of the dark side, it will require resisting the poison of extrabiblical, unrealistic, legalistic expectations in favor of God's liberating grace. We will need to identify the numerous sources of the expectations that bind us and then soundly reject them. Be warned. It will not be an easy task for those who have lived under their weight for many years, as Charles Swindoll suggests:

Being free, enjoying your liberty, and allowing others the same enjoyment is hard to do if you're insecure. It is especially hard to do if you were raised by legalistic parents and led by legalistic pastors with an oversensitive conscience toward pleasing everyone. Those kinds of parents and pastors can be ultra-controlling, manipulative, and judgmental. Frequently they use the Bible as a hammer to pound folks into submission rather than as a guide to lead others to grace. Sometimes it takes years for people who have been under a legalistic cloud to finally have the courage to walk freely in the grace of God.[4]

Though the task may not be easy, applying the oil of grace to our lives will result in a measure of joy and freedom that will help us provide the kind of balanced leadership that will honor God, draw others to Christ, and fulfill us as leaders.

Targeting Insights

- The third step toward overcoming your dark side is to resist the poison of unrealistic expectations.
- Expectations are a two-edged sword either propelling you to achieve or weighing you down in failure. The unrealistic ones produce friction and pressure in your life that eventually lead to burnout.
- Applying the oil of God's grace to your life and leadership is the only sure way to liberate yourself from the poison of unrealistic expectations.

Applying Insights

1. Have you ever felt the burden of too many or too high expectations? If so, describe some of them.

2. What feelings did such expectations spawn?

3. Are you laboring under unrealistic expectations in your life at this moment? What are they? How do they fit into what you have identified as your dark side?

4. What do you believe God expects of you in your present situation, and how do those expectations compare to those you listed in your answer above?

5. How can you apply the oil of grace to your situation? What action can you take today to relieve some of the expectations in your life? See Matthew 11:28–30; Colossians 2:16–23.

18

STEP 4:
PRACTICE PROGRESSIVE
SELF-KNOWLEDGE

In addition to the previous three steps, gaining any measure of control over our dark side will involve the ongoing process of gathering knowledge about ourselves through the practice of specific disciplines and the use of certain tools. These disciplines and tools will provide us with a constant stream of information about ourselves that we can use in an effort to understand ourselves and overcome our dark side rather than passively being controlled by it.

Spiritual Disciplines

One of the most troubling realities about spiritual leaders today is the increasing number of them who do not consistently devote time to personal spiritual disciplines. Too many leaders today do not regularly expose themselves to the scrutinizing probe of the Holy Spirit by looking into Scripture.

Scripture Reading

According to the apostle James, through Scripture we can gain the accurate self-knowledge so necessary to the exercise of successful leadership.

> But prove yourselves doers of the word, and not merely hearers who delude themselves. For if anyone is a hearer of the word and not a doer, he is like a man who looks at his natural face in a mirror; for once he has looked at himself and gone away, he has immediately forgotten what kind of person he was. But one who looks intently at the perfect law, the law of liberty, and abides by it, not having become a forgetful hearer but an effectual doer, this man will be blessed in what he does.
>
> James 1:22–25

How easy it is to forget what kind of person we really are when we neglect the mirror of Scripture. The reason for our neglect is that our image as reflected by the holy mirror is not often flattering. It forces us to deal with the realities of our depravity and the dark side it has spawned. How much more comfortable it is to live in denial of our true nature! We must realize that consistent exposure to Scripture will provide us with the most accurate self-knowledge available to us.

Personal Retreats

Another aspect of spiritual discipline for any Christian leader is a periodic personal retreat. It is vital to step away from the busyness of ministry and leadership responsibilities to reflect on our own spiritual condition. Where have we grown sloppy in our Christian life? What have we been neglecting? What is the current condition of our most important relationships? How well have we been managing our time? What does God want to say to us and how would he like to direct us as the leader of his people? These are all issues that can be addressed in the context of a personal retreat.

Such retreats should be regularly scheduled for at least a twenty-four-hour period at a location that provides maximum privacy and solitude. Very often local monasteries and retreat centers provide a very nice and inexpensive location for such a purpose. It is important, if the retreat is to serve its purpose, that we approach our retreat day with an agenda so that we don't simply sleep away the day. A helpful tool for planning such a retreat can be found in *How to Conduct a Spiritual Life Retreat* by Norman Shawchuck, Reuben Job, and Robert Doherty (The Upper Room, 1986). Of particular interest are chapters 4 and 6 on the personally guided retreat and the private retreat.

It is difficult to overestimate the value of this important discipline in the leader's life. Even Jesus during a busy ministry schedule with a limited amount of time to accomplish his tasks was committed to regular times alone with God. The Gospels speak often of Jesus going away to a quiet place to be with his Father. If Christ disciplined himself in this way, how much more important that we do the same.

Devotional Reading

Another spiritual discipline that can save us many heartaches and prevent many problems in our exercise of leadership is devotional reading, written by spiritual leaders who have gone before us. This is not just reading theological tomes or novels by Christian authors, but focusing on the writings of Christian leaders, telling how God has worked in and through their lives, in an effort to see how God may want to work in ours as well. The writings of Richard Baxter, Watchman Nee, Eugene Peterson, E. Stanley Jones, Thomas à Kempis, Henri Nouwen, Charles Swindoll, and many others provide the developing leader with a wealth of lessons to be learned, practices to begin, and mistakes to avoid. This devotional reading should be a part of the leader's daily routine.

Journaling

The practice of keeping a journal involves putting one's life down on paper . . . as a clarifying process: "Who am I? What am I doing and why? How do I feel about my life, my world? In what ways am I growing or changing?"[1]

If there is one thing leaders need as they pursue self-knowledge and understanding, it is the ability to clarify the fears, motives, insecurities, and other emotions that lurk deep beneath the surface of their public leadership persona. Keeping a journal forces us to be honest with ourselves. It is possibly the only place where we can truly be ourselves, warts and all. In our journal we can finally explore our inner rumblings and give definition and shape to them. The safe confines of our journal can help us admit to feelings of jealousy, selfishness, and pride. Within these therapeutic pages we can feel free to identify those inner urges and compulsions that drive us. The simple act of placing them on paper, in black and white, reduces their power over us to some degree.

Additionally, it is in my journal that I practice a visual form of the spiritual composting process. During my regular time of spiritual disciplines, when particular Scripture passages alert me to aspects of my personality that still need significant change, I will turn to a page in the back of my journal that I have labeled "My Spiritual Compost Pile." There, using colored ink, I will write out whatever it is that is in need of spiritual composting.

On other occasions, as God points out areas of sin or character traits that are in need of forgiveness or transformation, I will again turn to my spiritual compost page and write them down in a different color ink, somewhat overlapping the previous entries. Eventually, what began as an ugly blot on the page, reminding me of my ongoing need to be shaped into the image of Christ, ends up being a unique, inky tapestry of sorts that actually has a measure of beauty. By the time I am ready to retire that particular journal and begin another one, my compost page is a reminder that God is in the constant process of redeeming my dark side and integrating the less desirable aspects of my personhood into a more spiritually formed whole.

If you have followed the steps in chapters 15–17 to overcome your dark side, your journal can then be the place where you become intimately acquainted with yourself, a type of spiritual autobiography. However, your journal will only be helpful to the degree that you are honest with yourself. It is important to remember as you keep a journal that the river of self-deceit and denial runs so deep and swift that your initial attempts to ford it may end in getting swept away by the current. There will be a constant temptation to paint yourself in the most favorable light. The urge will be strong to simply leave out some of your uglier and more negative behaviors and actions. When you succumb to these urges, you are being swept away by the current of self-denial and deceit. Just the act of journaling will not be helpful if you cannot be honest and probe your inner recesses. But rather than becoming discouraged and quitting, you need to persist until you are finally able to walk through the depths.

As we have seen, spiritual disciplines include more than just a brief reading of a prepared devotional guide. The disciplines also include personal retreats, devotional reading, journaling, and extended periods of prayer and fasting when appropriate. All of these provide extended opportunity for the Lord to work in the leader's life.

Many leaders, however, argue that they don't have time to maintain such a regimen of disciplines. They don't feel they can justify taking a full day or two each month for something as "luxurious" as a personal retreat. The simple truth is that these disciplines are not supplemental to what we do as spiritual leaders; they are the very core of who we are and what we do. Without a steady diet of such disciplines the effectiveness of our spiritual leadership is greatly reduced. If we are too busy for such things, we are clearly just too busy! It is time that we place a priority on what is truly important and not allow ourselves to be in bondage to the urgent. Some of the hardest work we will ever do will be during our time of personal retreat as we wrestle with God concerning issues in our life and the life of our church. Unfortunately this difficult work is becoming increasingly unpopular among the contemporary clergy intent on building the next megachurch. But it should not surprise us that as these disciplines become less important and more infrequently practiced, the rate of leadership failures will increase.

Other Tools

Personality Profiles and Tests

Another way we can gain invaluable self-knowledge is through the use of various profiles and tests that will help us see certain weaknesses in our personality and leadership style and offer encouraging suggestions to prevent us from falling victim to the various elements of our dark side. The following are some suggested profiles and tests:

1. *The Gallup Strengths Finder.* This tool assesses your top five personality strengths, indicating how God has hardwired you.
2. *Taylor Johnson Temperament Analysis* (TJTA). This is primarily a personality profile that plots your personality on a continuum in relation to eight different personality traits.
3. *Myers-Briggs.* This instrument is a personality profile and leadership profile. It helps leaders understand why they are attracted to certain types of leadership opportunities and identifies where they will be most effective.
4. *DiSC Personal Profile System.* The DiSC test helps identify primary and secondary leadership styles. It also points

out the inherent weaknesses in each leadership style and suggests potential defenses against being victimized by these weaknesses.

5. *Minnesota Multiphasic Personality Inventory* (MMPI). Unlike the previous tools, which can be self-administered, the MMPI must be administered by a professional. However, it can be helpful in pointing out aspects of mental and emotional functioning that could be serious impairments.

These tests can reveal such things as the tendency to influence others to the point of manipulating them in an effort to carry out our goals. They can reveal a need to please others or proneness to compulsive overwork. They point out the tendency to become defensive when criticized and the fear of taking risks in leadership. Though they cannot tell us why we struggle with these things, just being aware that we do struggle with them is half the battle. As new issues are revealed from the periodic utilization of these tests, we can reflect on the reasons they may be issues for us.

The use of these or similar tools is essential to self-knowledge. In addition to exposing our weaknesses, they also reveal our strengths. As we become more familiar with our gifts and God-given strengths, we can have confidence in our leadership and avoid displays of false humility and other self-deprecating behaviors. (For further information regarding these tools, refer to appendix A.)

Professional Counseling and Therapy

If you have taken the time and effort required to adequately plumb the depths of your past and have identified any childhood or adolescent experiences that may be dictating your behavior today; and if you have accepted the reality that you do indeed possess a dark side, no matter where on the continuum from mild to acute it falls; and if you have taken the steps to address your past the best that you are able; yet you still find no relief from or control over your dark side, it is probably an indication that you need some objective outside help.

A professional counselor or therapist may be able to supply the help you need. Leaders tend to think, however, that they do not need such help and that they can work through their struggles on their own. Pastors have no problem referring parishioners to counseling, often lauding the benefits that can be gained, yet they are often hesitant to access this very helpful source themselves. There are several reasons for this reluctance, most of which are a direct result of the dark side at work.

One of the most insidious aspects of the dark side is that it can maintain its presence in our lives without completely disabling us. Even when the struggle is with something as severe as manic-depression, the depressions are seldom so enduring that they prevent all normal function. At the peak of a manic episode there can be such feelings of energy, creativity, and productivity that professional help hardly seems necessary. Even in the darkness of a depressive crevasse that inevitably follows such periods of manic activity, it is not easy to seek help because there is the feeling that this too will pass.

Unfortunately there are some Christian circles that still insist on dismissing out of hand the usefulness of any form of professional counseling, choosing instead to label everything that ails us as the product of sin that simply needs to be confessed. Obviously every area of human weakness is ultimately the result of the Fall and the depravity spawned by it. That does not stop us, however, from getting corrective lenses when we are nearsighted or having surgical procedures when they are warranted. This simplistic philosophy cannot be biblically supported and should not hinder the leader who needs professional help from seeking it.

Spiritual leaders also fear that their engagement of a professional counselor or therapist will send the wrong message to parishioners and those they lead. Who wants to be led by someone who cannot solve his or her own problems? How can we expect people to come to us for help and spiritual guidance once they discover that we need help and guidance ourselves? The reverse is often what people think, however. Rather than dissuading those we lead and serve from coming to us for help, their discovery of our use of a trained helper may actually remove many of the barriers that inhibit them from coming to us. If we have found the need to seek help, surely it is all right if they seek help as well.

Before we ever find our way to the counselor's office, we will need to be committed to three important, Christlike qualities. First, we will need to demonstrate humility. We will need to admit that we are not capable of solving all of our own problems. Second, we will need to demonstrate transparency. Seeking the objective input and help of another person will require the ability to reveal the inner recesses of our life. It will necessitate sharing our weaknesses, fears, and failures, something not always easily done by the personality types who have achieved leadership status. It is essential nonetheless. Finally, it will demand honesty. Even if we should wander into a counselor's office, we will not be helped if we refuse to be honest. It is crucial to note that there is a distinct difference between transparency and honesty. Transparency has to do with the depth and nature of our self-revelations. Honesty, on the other hand, has to do with the accuracy of what we reveal. The leader who exhibits these qualities and seeks the aid of a professional helper is well on the way to disarming his or her dark side.

Personal Accountability Groups

Leaders seem to have a natural aversion to scrutiny and criticism. Ironically it is our ability to open ourselves to close scrutiny and even criticism that often serves us best in our efforts to avoid the destructive effects of the dark side.

Dr. John Maxwell, popular author and lecturer in the area of leadership, has stated that one of the greatest contributing factors to the recent moral failure of numerous spiritual leaders has been their unwillingness to submit themselves to ongoing accountable relationships.[2] Richard Dortch, who received a federal prison sentence for his role in Jim Bakker's failed PTL ministry, has stated, "Accountability sometimes can be perfunctory and shallow. Submission goes a step further and says, 'I'm willing to turn loose the control of the vision.'"[3] When a leader is finally willing to submit to accountable relationships, according to Dortch, it "means pursuing the vision with such transparency that we *gladly* invite the world to look at our books. Pride can't get far when we work out the financing and operation of our vision with absolute integrity."[4]

It is critical to the effectiveness of our accountable relationships that we be transparent so that we can keep our dark side in check. On the other hand, even when we maintain accountable relationships, it is possible for us to withhold important information and subtle motives that hinder our accountability group from performing their task. We need to subject our goals and motives to much more than a superficial inspection by those we count on to hold us accountable to biblical principles and godly leadership practices.

We need to recognize that there are three levels of openness to accountability and input from others: level one is simply not objecting to advice; level two is wanting advice; and level three is actually seeking out advice.[5] If our accountable relationships are ever going to serve their purpose, we must move to level three, where we eagerly seek out the advice of trusted advisors.

Who, you might ask, should compose our accountability group? This should be a group of seasoned, spiritually growing people whom you trust and who love you and have your best interests at heart. Once you identify three to five individuals meeting this description, you can ask them if they would be interested in serving you in this manner. It is important to let them know you are serious about this process and to define the role you want them to play. We suggest writing a covenant of sorts that covers the group's purpose, your intentions to submit to the group's consensus on questionable matters, confidentiality, and the manner in which you will utilize their service. (See appendix B for an example of an accountability group covenant.) This process will reduce the possibility of frustration and disappointment on the part of all members.

Once this group of individuals has agreed to help you, use them. Use them when you are dealing with difficult decisions, determining directions for your life and ministry, navigating through controversial waters, or struggling with inner feelings regarding various issues. Give them permission to ask you probing questions at any time as a means of keeping you on the straight and narrow in your exercise of leadership.

Formal Performance Evaluations

One final tool that every leader should take full advantage of is the process of formal performance evaluations by those over him or her. In many church settings the senior pastor is never formally reviewed by the church board or those in authority over him. Too many leaders are allowed to ignore their weaknesses year after year without ever being informed of areas that need improvement.

Though opening oneself to formal evaluation is always a risky and frightening experience, it is well worth the risk and fear it engenders. The reality is that others usually see the effects of our dark side long before we do. When we open ourselves to evaluation, we have the opportunity to address potential problem areas in their early stages before they get out of control. It is always painful to acknowledge our failures and problems but it is absolutely essential if we are ever to gain control of our dark side.

What should you do if you are in an environment that does not currently provide formal performance evaluations? Our suggestion is that you approach a board chairman or other person you are responsible to and strongly express your desire for annual written reviews. Once the board recovers from the shock, they no doubt will agree to assist you. If the leaders you are responsible to do not have the resources or knowledge to conduct such a review, take the responsibility to provide them with some guidelines and examples that will help them as they design a procedure. We have found an annual performance review to be not only challenging but also extremely encouraging and humbling as we see the ways God is effectively using us. Submitting to an annual performance review can provide a leader with years' worth of self-knowledge that can be used to exercise better control over his or her dark side. (For an example of a pastoral performance evaluation, refer to appendix D.)

Knowledge Is Power

The more knowledge we gain about ourselves, the better able we are to overcome our dark side. As long as we choose to live in ignorance of our unique weaknesses and dysfunctions, we will continue to be victimized by them. With increased knowledge will come the increased power to live a life of balance, free from the destructive effects of our dark side.

TARGETING INSIGHTS

- The fourth step toward overcoming your dark side is to practice the discipline of self-knowledge.
- Overcoming the dark side of leadership requires regular exposure to the mirror of Scripture, as it will provide you with the most accurate self-knowledge available (James 1:22–25).
- The practice of spiritual disciplines will likely include regular reading of and meditation on Scripture, periods of meditation and reflection, devotional reading and prayer, and extended spiritual retreats.

APPLYING INSIGHTS

1. Do you practice a regular time of Scripture reading beyond preparation for preaching or teaching?

    ___ Yes ___ No

If not, what step could you take to do so?

2. Do you take time weekly or monthly for meditation and reflection on Scripture, God, or your life?

____ Yes ____ No

If not, what would need to change in your life to allow time for meditation?

3. Do you occasionally read a devotional classic or contemporary devotional material simply to feed your soul?

____ Yes ____ No

If not, try a biography of a Christian leader. Begin reading a chapter a week.

4. Do you have regular time for prayer outside of meals, church gatherings, or formal ministry settings?

____ Yes ____ No

If not, what seems to keep you from praying more?

5. Do you take an extended time for spiritual reflection, such as a retreat, once or twice a year?

____ Yes ____ No

If not, look over your calendar today and schedule a personal retreat within the next six months.

6. Do you keep a journal in which you enter your deepest thoughts, dreams, passions, failures, and victories?

____ Yes ____ No

If not, go to a stationery store, purchase a notebook, and write in it tonight.

7. Do you take advantage of the opportunity to know yourself better through personality profiles and tests?

   ___ Yes ___ No

   If not, choose one of the suggested profiles and use it as a means of gaining insight into your personality (see appendix A).

8. Do you have a group of people with whom you meet and are able to be honest and transparent and who hold you accountable for your dark side?

   ___ Yes ___ No

   If not, list two or three people you would feel comfortable meeting with. Talk to them about meeting as a group, beginning next week.

9. Do you participate in a formal evaluation process with other leaders in your organization?

   ___ Yes ___ No

   If not, ask your main leadership board to develop a formal evaluation process this year (see appendix D).

10. Do you take advantage of continuing education opportunities, such as seminars, workshops, or degree programs?

    ___ Yes ___ No

    What areas of continuing education would interest you?

The ideas given above and throughout this chapter are not meant to burden your already busy schedule. Instead of trying to add several of them to what you are already doing, consider increasing your time commitment to those already in your schedule or adding just one idea for now. What will you do?

19

STEP 5:
UNDERSTAND YOUR
IDENTITY IN CHRIST

Ultimately all of the previous four steps will leave us feeling frustrated and empty if we do not understand and accept our true identity in Jesus Christ. We must come to the point where we recognize that our value is not dependent on our performance, position, titles, achievements, or the power that we wield. Rather, our worth exists independently of anything we have ever done or will do in the future. Without the grace of God that is found only in his son, Jesus Christ, as Isaiah the prophet declared, our best efforts and most altruistic acts are like filthy rags in God's sight (Isa. 64:6). Everything we might learn about our dark side will be without significant benefit if we fail to find our value in Christ.

213

Worthy in Christ

In the final analysis we must always remember that our greatest source of worth as leaders should come from the knowledge that we are known by God and declared righteous in Christ. All other posturing will leave us wanting. As we follow the previous steps of reflection and gaining self-knowledge, there can be a boomerang effect of sorts if the results are not carefully viewed against the backdrop of God's grace and our position in Christ. Personal introspection of any serious nature will always reveal that we are bottomless pits of need and depravity apart from Christ. But with Christ, there is hope for us.

We are told in the Bible that there are two sources of life. One is earthly; the other heavenly. One is physical; the other spiritual. One ultimately leads to death; the other to eternal life. We have both a condition and a position, or a state here on earth and a standing before God. Our first birth provided us with a physical body and placed us in a sinful condition on this earth. The new birth presents us with a new life (eventually a new body) and places us in a holy position in heaven.

Position (Standing)	Condition (State)
In heaven	On earth
Spiritual	Physical
Life	Death

The question is, from which source do we derive our value as people? As leaders?

Our worth as God's people is what results from our *position* in Christ rather than our *condition* on earth. Christian growth takes place as we appropriate what we already are in Christ (our position) by faith and then practice that in our earthly lives (our condition). For example, our condition is that we are Christians growing in maturity. Hopefully most of us are progressing in our walk with Christ, reflecting his attributes increasingly. Of course since we are not perfect, we will and do make mistakes and experience failure and struggles. If

214

we look at our earthly state to receive our worth, then we certainly will be disappointed. However, if we concentrate on what we actually are in our standing before God, we will discover that we are valuable! Walking by faith means that we live according to truth, not by feelings. At times we may indeed feel worthless. But to concentrate on our condition means we are not living by faith. Even in times of defeat or frustration or failure, as we walk by faith not by sight, we can know that we are valuable because of our standing with God in heaven.

While there are numerous biblical passages that illustrate our position and condition, we will cite only a few. We have highlighted the words that reflect our position in Christ. "Therefore if anyone is *in Christ*, he is a *new creature;* the old things passed away; behold, *new things have come*" (2 Cor. 5:17, emphasis ours); and "For as in Adam all die, so also *in Christ all will be made alive*" (1 Cor. 15:22, emphasis ours). A brief survey of Ephesians chapter 1 is enough to lift the spirits of even the most self-critical leader. In it Paul reminds us not of our condition but of our position!

> [God] *chose us in Him* [Christ] before the foundation of the world, that *we would be holy and blameless before Him.* In love He *predestined us to adoption as sons* through Jesus Christ to Himself, according to the kind intention of His will. . . . *In Him we have redemption* through His blood, *the forgiveness of our trespasses, according to the riches of His grace, which He lavished on us.*
>
> Ephesians 1:4–5, 7–8, emphasis ours

Paul declares that we have been chosen by God himself, declared holy and blameless, and completely forgiven. He goes on to say that we have obtained an eternal inheritance (Eph. 1:11) and have been sealed by the Holy Spirit of God (Eph. 1:13), which serves as his guarantee of these amazing benefits.

In Romans we are told by Paul that "the Spirit Himself testifies with our spirit that *we are children of God,* and if children, heirs also, *heirs of God and fellow heirs with Christ*" (Rom. 8:16–17, emphasis ours).

In his letter to the rambunctious church at Corinth Paul reminds us that Jesus Christ is our wisdom, righteousness, sanctification, and redemption (1 Cor. 1:30). In Philippians we can find confidence with Paul that "He who began *a good work in you* will perfect it until the day of Christ Jesus" (Phil. 1:6). Our benefits in Christ are noted in the following chart.

Position (Standing)	Condition (State)
In heaven	On earth
Spiritual	Physical
Life	Death
New birth	First birth
New man	Old man
New nature	Old nature
New creature	Old creature
Justified	Condemned
Forgiven	Guilty
In Christ	In Adam

Over and over again the Scriptures remind us that we are no longer the same person that was born to our earthly parents. We have been made new spiritual creatures by the power of God. Yet we were all valuable to God even before we were in Christ by faith. "For while we were still helpless, at the right time Christ died for the ungodly. For one will hardly die for a righteous man; though perhaps for the good man someone would dare even to die. But *God demonstrates His own love toward us*, in that *while we were yet sinners*, Christ died for us" (Rom. 5:6–8).

It is not our achievements and organizational successes that give us a lasting sense of worth—it is Jesus Christ. Though our leadership efforts do have value both now and in the future, they do not imbue us with value.

Our Choice

When we choose to live in ignorance of our dark side and resist all attempts to understand ourselves, our spiritual adversary is able to keep us in bondage through a continuous flow of lies and deception. Through our blinded eyes we are able to see ourselves only in our present condition.

In contrast, as we begin to take the aforementioned steps and learn about ourselves, we are better able to take these issues to Jesus and find complete release. God blows away the clouds and lets us see our position in Christ! If we fail to understand those unmet needs and existential debts that are driving us, it is more difficult to apply the truth of God's Word to them and find freedom from them. Any attempts to overcome the dark side apart from the application of spiritual truth about our true position and identity in Christ will end in failure.

As part of this step, we highly recommend reading Neil Anderson's books *Victory over the Darkness* and *The Bondage Breaker*. (See the suggested reading list for additional information.) These books will enable driven leaders to find ultimate value in their identity in Christ, apart from their performance and achievement.

A Lifelong Process

Overcoming our dark side is not an event, it is a lifelong process that every leader must be continually working through. As we gain a progressively deeper understanding of our dark side and consistently practice the steps necessary to redeem it, we can protect ourselves and those we love from the painful, humiliating, and often devastating failures produced by the dark side.

TARGETING INSIGHTS

- The fifth step toward overcoming your dark side is to understand your identity in Christ.

- Your true value does not reside in your performance, position, titles, achievement, or power (your condition on earth). It exists independently of anything you have done or will do.
- Your greatest source of worth is being known by God and declared righteous in Christ (your position in heaven).

Applying Insights

1. What makes you feel like a person of worth? Name the specific actions, praise, work, or accomplishments that have brought you good feelings in the past.

2. Why do these things seem to provide you with feelings of worth?

3. Do your feelings of worth come from your position in Christ, actions, praise, work, accomplishments, or other aspects of your life?

4. Read Ephesians 1:3–14, replacing the words *us* and *we* with your own name or the personal pronoun *I*, and then explain how it makes you feel.

5. Begin building a new view of your worth by reading and reflecting on the following Scriptures once a day for the next week.

- Romans 8:16–17

- I Corinthians 1:26–31

- I Corinthians 3:4–9

- Galatians 3:26–29

- Ephesians 1:3–14

- Philippians 1:6

- Philippians 3:7–14

POSTSCRIPT

The dark side of leadership has profound implications both within the church and among the ranks of Christian leaders. Few things during the decade of the eighties tainted the world's view of Christianity as severely as the failure of several high-profile Christian leaders. The church today faces a leadership crisis of proportions similar to the one faced by Israel when the prophet Ezekiel declared:

> Woe, shepherds of Israel who have been feeding themselves! Should not the shepherds feed the flock? You eat the fat and clothe yourselves with the wool, you slaughter the fat sheep without feeding the flock. . . . They were scattered for lack of a shepherd, and they became food for every beast of the field and were scattered.
>
> Ezekiel 34:2–3, 5

Because Israel's spiritual leaders had failed to lead them properly and instead led for the satisfaction of their own personal needs, the people suffered. God did not allow this prostitution of leadership to go unpunished. Ezekiel also delivered God's message of judgment on these failed leaders:

> Behold, I am against the shepherds, and I will demand My sheep from them and make them cease from feeding sheep. So the shepherds will not feed themselves anymore, but I will deliver My flock from their mouth, so that they will not be food for them.
>
> Ezekiel 34:10

How easy it is for us as spiritual leaders to use our ministry positions and the people we have been called to lead to advance our own goals and meet our own neurotic needs. The constant flow of failures among Christian leaders today in every denomination threatens the fabric of the church of Jesus Christ. Our credibility is being eroded among the people we have been called to reach because scores of failures among Christian leaders have created a cynicism toward the church within our culture.

Our mission is in jeopardy if we cannot stem the tide of fallen leaders. It is crucial that the church address this issue before irreparable harm is done to the cause of Christ in this generation. We must help educate and alert young leaders to the dangers of their dark side. As important as the technical aspects of ministry are to success (e.g., exegesis, languages, theology, counseling), their ability to overcome the dark side of their personality is even more vital to effective ministry. If the leader fails in this crucial area, all other skills are reduced in value. Dealing openly, directly, and biblically with the dark side is crucial to the future health of the church and its ministry effectiveness in the world.

May God find us faithful.

PERSONALITY PROFILES

1. The Gallup Strengths Finder
   See http://gmj.gallup.com/book_center/strengthsfinder

2. Taylor Johnson Temperament Analysis® (TJTA®)
   For certification on the TJTA, contact:
   Psychological Publications, Inc.
   PO Box 3577
   Thousand Oaks, CA 91359-0577
   (800) 345-8378
   Fax (805) 373-1753

3. Myers-Briggs®
   See Isabel Briggs Myers, *Gifts Differing* (Palo Alto, CA:
   Consulting Psychologists Press, 1980).
   For certification to use the Myers-Briggs Type Indicator
   write or call:
   The Association for Psychological Type

9140 Ward Parkway
Kansas City, MO 64114
(816) 444-3500 or fax (816) 444-0330

4. DiSC® Personal Profile System®
Published by:
Carlson Learning Company
PO Box 1763
Minneapolis, MN 55440-9238
To order copies or to receive complete information on certification training, contact Dr. Gary L. McIntosh, PO Box 892589, Temecula, CA 92589-2589; phone or fax (951) 506-3086; email: cgnet@earthlink.net.

5. Minnesota Multiphasic Personality Inventory (MMPI)
For certification in MMPI use, one needs a master's degree in psychology or a related field with at least one semester course or equivalent specifically teaching the MMPI and its use. Contact your local college or university for further information.

ACCOUNTABILITY GROUP COVENANT

As a member of [name's] accountability group, I covenant to:

1. Meet with [name] once a month for the purpose of holding him or her accountable to his or her values and goals.

2. Ask probing questions based on the personal constitution [see appendix C] and goals [name] has given to me. I will also feel free to ask questions in any other area of his or her life and ministry.

3. Keep all conversations confidential.

4. Strongly challenge [name] in those areas where he or she is not living consistently with his or her values and engaging in behavior that mitigates the achievement of his or her goals.

5. Periodically call [name's] spouse to ensure that he or she is being truthful and accurately representing himself or herself during accountability meetings.

6. Pray for [name] and his or her faithfulness to God on the drive home from our meeting together.

As the person submitting myself to your accountability, I covenant to:

1. Be truthful in the answers given to all questions asked.

2. Pray for you on the drive to our accountability meeting.

3. Take to heart any counsel or recommendations you might give.

4. Be on time for all meetings, not monopolize your time beyond one and a half hours per meeting, and not call you needlessly between meetings.

Signed,

_____

(Name)   (Date)

_____

(Accountability group member)   (Date)

Sample Personal Constitution

Samuel D. Rima
January 20, 1994

I, Samuel D. Rima, promise with God's help to:

1. Maintain a growing and increasingly intimate conversational relationship with God.

   The single most important value I hold is a personal belief in a living, loving, personal, sovereign God. This God desires to know me and interact with me. I will be conscious of my relationship with God and place it above every other value or goal. I will avoid every influence and activity that undermines my relationship with God.

2. Love others as I love myself and always deal with them as I wish others would deal with me.

   I will strive to treat every person I deal with exactly as I would like to be treated. Every person is highly valued and loved by God regardless of his or her actions, attitudes, and struggles.

3. Build the church of Jesus Christ.

   My highest calling in life is to contribute to the growth and advancement of Christ's church on earth. The church is not an organization but a people united around the person and work of Jesus Christ. It is the most influential force in the world and is the world's only hope. Society and culture prosper to the degree that the church of Jesus Christ is healthy and growing.

4. Influence others to pursue a growing relationship with God.

   Spending one-on-one time with people is one of my most effective ways to influence them for Christ. It is also vital that I spend time with small groups of people to share my passion for Christ and his mission in the world. When I am with others, I will be conscious of the opportunity I have been given to influence them for Christ and his kingdom—I am his ambassador.

5. Love my wife as Christ loves the church.

   I will spend quality time with Sue to share my life with her and nurture her gifts and interests. I desire to see her be the most effective, fulfilled, and productive person she can possibly be. I will consider her interests above my own.

6. Love my children and deal with them as God deals with me, his child.

   I will be involved in the lives of my children. I will spend time with each of them on a monthly basis. I take full responsibility for their intellectual, emotional, spiritual, and physical development. My goal is to encourage them and demonstrate the unconditional love of God at all times.

7. Maintain a daily time of solitude for the purpose of spiritual growth.

Each day from 5:30 a.m. to 7:00 a.m. is my most important and nonnegotiable appointment of the day. It is a time when I explore myself and my relationship with God and seek his guidance and mind for the coming day. It is a time of reading, reflection, writing in my journal, prayer, and solitude.

8. Be trustworthy and a person of integrity.

I will be honest in all things and guard myself from exaggeration and lies of omission. I will admit when I have been wrong and seek forgiveness when necessary. I will foster trust with all those I work and interact with. I will not give people a reason to doubt my integrity. I will be accountable to a small group of select men on a regular basis.

9. Manage my time for maximum effectiveness.

I will keep a daily planner at all times. I will control the events of my life that are controllable. I will spend the first fifteen minutes of each day planning the events of that day in a way that will most effectively accomplish my goals. I will not waste time and procrastinate. My schedule and priorities will reflect and be consistent with my governing values and promote the achievement of my long-term goals.

10. Maintain my physical health, fitness, and appearance.

My body is the temple of the Holy Spirit of the living God and my only vehicle for accomplishing all that

229

God desires me to accomplish. Thus I will employ self-control in my eating habits. I will exercise at least five times a week and keep my weight under 180 pounds. I will give special attention to my personal appearance and look my best.

11. Provide for my family's financial future.

    I will spend less than I earn. I will save each month to provide emergency cash reserves. I will contribute monthly to a retirement vehicle that will maximize my investment. I will work toward a home environment that is free from financially induced pressures. I will not use consumer credit for things I cannot pay for in full at the end of the month.

12. Grow intellectually and professionally.

    I will read on a daily basis and will select my reading from a variety of subjects and formats representing the best reading available. I will pursue my doctoral degree and participate in regular continuing education seminars for the purpose of intellectual and professional stimulation. I cannot teach from a stagnant pool.

13. Communicate with excellence and make the most of every opportunity to speak before a group.

    I will prepare exhaustively for each opportunity I am given to communicate. I will never attempt to "wing it" in any setting. I will give my best possible effort. If I cannot speak with genuine conviction and passion, I will not speak at all.

14. Always see things as they can be, not simply as they are.

    Every goal is a planned conflict with the status quo. Things can always be better than they are and I will promote their betterment. I will communicate vision for the future with excitement and enthusiasm but will not manipulate others to make that vision a reality. If I cannot convince people to follow willingly, the vision is not worth being followed.

15. Leave everything I am involved with better than when I began.

    I will add value to the people, projects, and organizations I am involved with. I will not be a user but a contributor; not a complainer but an encourager. I will be a problem solver and not a problem reporter.

APPENDIX D

SAMPLE PERFORMANCE
EVALUATION

SAMUEL D. RIMA
MARCH 2, 1996

Pastor Rima has completed three years of ministry at Bethany Baptist Church. The following comments reflect the collective views of the church board concerning his performance during the past year.

Preaching/Teaching: Pastor Rima is an excellent preacher. He is articulate, well prepared, and makes good use of examples. His sermons are challenging, convicting, relevant, meaningful, powerful, and motivational. People get taught many lessons for life's situations. He makes himself vulnerable by using personal examples to make a point. He builds his sermons around Scripture, and the action steps at the conclusion of the message are both pertinent and practical.

Some services may get a little long, but this may be corrected by cutting back some on preliminary activities, music, etc. It may be a reasonable goal to generally conclude the service by 11:15. Special music selections should normally be a part of the service.

Leadership: Pastor Rima is a very strong leader. He is aggressive, persuasive, and a good motivator and planner. He does a good job of touching base with individual board members between board meetings. He is well prepared for meetings. He is confident in his abilities and thinks through his positions well before attempting to convince others. He has excellent visionary skills.

When Pastor Rima really feels strongly about an issue, it is difficult for him to back off when the board or other leaders wish to go in another direction. He can also take things too personally at times. In addition, Pastor Rima needs to be careful about telling people about conversations with others (naming individuals) when it's not necessary to do so.

Communications: This is another strength of Pastor Rima's, both in written and verbal communications. He is sensitive to what is needed, including how much and how often. He is clear and articulate and desires the congregation to be informed of pertinent matters as opposed to being secretive. The Harvest 2000 plan is excellent and is predicated on keeping the congregation informed of relocation and ministry activities. He is excellent on his feet in responding to a variety of issues.

Congregational Relationships: Pastor Sam can relate well to all ages and groups of people. He is a solution seeker with members presenting difficult situations to handle. Although he likely does not have the gift of mercy, he does express empathy toward others. He is good at working toward attracting newcomers to

234

the church. He can relate to people in many different ways (hunting, fishing, planning retreats, social outings, etc.).

Although Pastor Rima is good with relationships with all people, he is more attracted to certain types of people (potential leaders, progressive thinkers, those open to change, etc.). Tom Backer provides a good balance and probably fills a void in certain areas of dealing with individuals whose concerns may be more "petty."

Management of Staff: Pastor Rima provides good vision, positive direction, and builds a sense of loyalty among the staff. He does not appear to be continually looking over their shoulder but at the same time provides appropriate guidance. He challenges them to think "outside the box" and gives them exposure to the congregation on Sunday mornings (announcements, prayer, occasional preaching, etc.).

Although not a noted problem, Pastor Rima needs to be careful so that his strong personality does not thwart concepts and ideas from his staff. An analysis should be made to determine if board meetings can be accommodated so that Brian Allen can attend.

Administrative Functions: The administrative functions are handled very well. Pastor Rima is well organized, focused, efficient, and capable of doing many different things well. He is well prepared for meetings, presentations, etc.

Pastor Rima has a tendency to do too much himself. He has a strong desire to be in control, which is a reflection of his strong personality. He has perfectionistic tendencies that may result in his actually performing administrative duties at a level higher than what is required to do a very good job.

Other: Pastor Rima is very good at counseling and conflict resolution. He is good at focusing on the relevance of programs the church offers. His gift for vision and change are needed at Bethany. At the same time, his perseverance in the face of opposition is necessary at times as well. Consideration should be given to some form of board members/spouse Bible study/ training when new board members are in place.

Major Accomplishments: Some of the accomplishments during the past year include the following:

- Entire relocation process—ability to get complacent church members who are set in their ways to vote for relocation.
- Highest attendance and giving on record.
- Leading the church program away from traditional but ineffective programming, such as Sunday night services to Home Groups and revamped ABFs.
- Continued leadership in revising the morning worship service.
- Staff policy manual.
- Inclusion of two board members at the Maxwell Conference in Denver.
- Achieving of doctorate.

Areas of Improvement: Potential areas of improvement are as follows:

- Continued ongoing review of balance of spiritual, physical, and family life.
- Work on delegating more and controlling less.
- Develop more strengths in areas of weakness (empathy, visiting the sick, patience, etc.).
- Improve driving skills to stay out of the ditch (just kidding).

Summary: The purpose of a performance appraisal is to show an individual his or her strengths and weaknesses. Each of us has both. At the same time it is important to look at strengths relative to weaknesses. With regard to Pastor Rima, the strengths far outweigh the weaknesses. He is the best minister we have worked with and has an excellent blend of preaching and communication skills, vision, administrative abilities, drive, and concern for others. Most important, he believes in prayer and bases his beliefs on Scripture. We hope we can keep him at Bethany for a long time.

IDENTIFYING YOUR
DARK SIDE

As our dark side develops over our lifetime—the results of our unique family of origin, traumatic experiences, and the way we processed them—it begins to take on a specific shape. The various characteristics of the dark side can be grouped into some broad categories. Even though these five categories may not account for every possible related issue we face, they can provide the general framework we need to begin the process of understanding and overcoming our unique dark side.

Giving Shape to Our Dark Side

Below you will find twelve groups of five statements lettered A through E. Each question has a possible range of responses. Read each statement and circle the number that most closely corresponds to your impressions of yourself. If you are serious about identifying your dark side and intent on preventing significant failure in your leadership, it is absolutely vital that you answer each question as honestly as possible. Again, remember as you respond that the current of self-deception and denial runs deep and swift in our lives. We will be tempted to respond to some less flattering questions in ways that we wish were true, but deep down we know they are not. If we succumb to this temptation, our dark side is victimizing us. Let's begin.

Scoring Guide

1 = strongly disagree   2 = disagree   3 = uncertain   4 = agree   5 = strongly agree

Group 1

A. I find myself resisting standards and procedures for formal review of my performance. 1 2 3 4 5

B. I often worry that my superiors do not approve of the quality of my work. 1 2 3 4 5

C. When I see two key leaders of my organization discreetly talking, I worry that they may be talking about me. 1 2 3 4 5

D. Fellow leaders in my church or organization frequently question whether my proposed goals and projects are feasible and realistic. 1 2 3 4 5

E. I grew up in a family with one or more substance-dependent people (alcoholics, drug addicts, food addicts, etc.). 1 2 3 4 5

Group 2

A. It is common for me to procrastinate on major projects that I must do. 1 2 3 4 5

B. I am highly regimented in my daily personal routines such as exercise schedule or spiritual disciplines. 1 2 3 4 5

C. It really bothers me to think about my board or leadership team meeting without me being present. 1 2 3 4 5

D. I am obsessed with knowing how others feel about my performance. 1 2 3 4 5

E. I grew up in a strict, legalistic religious environment that held its members to an unrealistic standard of behavior and discouraged open, honest communication about personal problems and struggles. 1 2 3 4 5

1 = strongly disagree   2 = disagree   3 = uncertain   4 = agree   5 = strongly agree

Group 3

A. I regularly resist others' ideas that could translate into increased performance or responsibility for me.   1 2 3 4 5

B. When circumstances dictate that I must interrupt my daily personal routines, I find myself feeling out of sorts and even guilty for having "skipped" a day.   1 2 3 4 5

C. When an associate receives rave reviews for a project or some special assignment, I experience intense jealousy rather than joy in the success and recognition he or she is receiving.   1 2 3 4 5

D. I find it difficult to receive criticism of any kind, reacting with anger, anxiety, or even depression when it does come.   1 2 3 4 5

E. I am usually willing to put up with or ignore bizarre, embarrassing, or inappropriate behavior in others.   1 2 3 4 5

Group 4

A. I find myself constantly performing beneath my capabilities.   1 2 3 4 5

B. I frequently find myself conscious of my status in relationship to others.   1 2 3 4 5

C. I require subordinates and associates within my organization to provide me with detailed reports of their activities.   1 2 3 4 5

D. At times I find myself thinking, *I'll show them; they could never make it around here without me,* when I experience conflict situations or opposition to my proposals and plans.   1 2 3 4 5

E. I often refrain from sharing my opinion in a group setting until I have heard the opinions of others in the group.   1 2 3 4 5

Group 5

A. I experience periodic but regular outbursts of anger and frustration that are just within the bounds of what is considered acceptable behavior.   1 2 3 4 5

B. It is difficult for me to take an unplanned day off from work responsibilities just to goof around or spend some time with friends or family, feeling like a "slacker" if I do.   1 2 3 4 5

C. I struggle when an associate, rather than me, is asked to take on a high-profile special assignment or project.   1 2 3 4 5

D. In spite of achieving what others would consider significant success, I still find myself dissatisfied and driven to achieve greater things in an effort to feel good about myself.   1 2 3 4 5

E. I frequently worry about hurting people's feelings by sharing my true feelings and thoughts.   1 2 3 4 5

241

1 = strongly disagree   2 = disagree   3 = uncertain   4 = agree   5 = strongly agree

Group 6

A. Occasionally I intentionally forget suggested projects.   1 2 3 4 5

B. While away from work, I still find myself thinking about work-related topics, often sitting down to write out my ideas at length, even if it disrupts family activities.   1 2 3 4 5

C. I have few intimate or meaningful relationships within my church or organization and find myself avoiding such relationships.   1 2 3 4 5

D. I am willing to bend rules and press the envelope of acceptable behavior in order to accomplish my goals.   1 2 3 4 5

E. I often feel responsible for problems I did not create.   1 2 3 4 5

Group 7

A. Sometimes I give others the silent treatment as an expression of my anger.   1 2 3 4 5

B. I like to plan the details of my vacations so I don't waste time or miss anything important.   1 2 3 4 5

C. I insist on absolute loyalty from those who work for me and prohibit staff from criticizing me in any way.   1 2 3 4 5

D. Deep down I find myself feeling jealous of the success and achievements of associates or organizations in my area or field of expertise.   1 2 3 4 5

E. I find it difficult to sleep because I worry about someone else's problems or behavior.   1 2 3 4 5

Group 8

A. I find myself telling others that nothing is bothering me when in reality I am seething inside.   1 2 3 4 5

B. I often explode in anger after being cut off while driving or after being irritated by other petty issues.   1 2 3 4 5

C. I often worry that there is a significant faction within my organization that would like to see me leave.   1 2 3 4 5

D. I am often unaware of or unconcerned about the financial pressures my goals and projects place on those I lead, my family, or the organization I serve.   1 2 3 4 5

E. I find myself frequently overcommitted and feel my life is out of control.   1 2 3 4 5

I = strongly disagree   2 = disagree   3 = uncertain   4 = agree   5 = strongly agree

Group 9

A. I tend to be generally pessimistic and feel negative about my future.   I 2 3 4 5

B. I am meticulous with my personal appearance, keeping shoes shined, clothes   I 2 3 4 5
perfectly pressed, hair carefully cut and groomed, and fingernails clipped.

C. I have probed people for what they know or for special information they may   I 2 3 4 5
have relating to certain leaders in my organization.

D. Success or failure in a project has a direct bearing on my self-image and sense   I 2 3 4 5
of personal worth.

E. I find it extremely difficult to say no to people even when I know that saying yes   I 2 3 4 5
will result in difficulty for me or my family.

Group 10

A. Others have expressed to me that I make them feel uncomfortable.   I 2 3 4 5

B. I frequently comment about the long hours I keep and my heavy workload but   I 2 3 4 5
am secretly proud of my "work ethic."

C. Those I work with often complain about my lack of a healthy sense of humor.   I 2 3 4 5

D. I am highly conscious of how colleagues and those to whom I am accountable   I 2 3 4 5
regard my accomplishments.

E. I constantly feel a sense of guilt but have difficulty identifying its source.   I 2 3 4 5

Group 11

A. Strategic planning and goal setting are difficult for me, and I resist such   I 2 3 4 5
exercises.

B. When another person makes sloppy errors or pays little attention to detail, I   I 2 3 4 5
become annoyed and judge him or her.

C. I routinely refer to those I lead as "my people" or "my organization," yet bristle   I 2 3 4 5
when the same designation is spoken by an associate.

D. I need to be recognized or "on top" when meeting with a group of fellow leaders   I 2 3 4 5
or associates.

E. I feel like I never measure up to those around me and have self-deprecating   I 2 3 4 5
thoughts.

243

1 = strongly disagree   2 = disagree   3 = uncertain   4 = agree   5 = strongly agree

Group 12

A. Sometimes I catch myself trying to manipulate others in group settings by venting my anger and emotions when facing initiatives I do not support.   1 2 3 4 5

B. I am obsessive about the smallest errors, worrying that they will reflect poorly on me.   1 2 3 4 5

C. I tend to take seriously even lighthearted comments and jokes directed at me, feeling there is probably a seed of truth in them.   1 2 3 4 5

D. I see myself as a nationally known figure at some time in the future or have plans to attain such a position.   1 2 3 4 5

E. When I receive compliments from others, I find it difficult to simply accept them without making qualifying statements.   1 2 3 4 5

Scoring Your Profile

To score your profile, go back through the groups of statements and total the scores for each letter. For example, total all of your A's, B's, etc., and place those totals in the spaces provided below. Once you have a total for all the letters, divide the total by five and round to the nearest whole number. Place that result in the Plotting column.

Statement Group	Total	Total divided by 5 and rounded to the nearest whole number	Plotting
A			
B			
C			
D			
E			

Dark Side Profile

To complete your dark side profile, take the number you placed in the Plotting column and transfer it onto the chart below on the appropriate axis. To do this, begin at the center of the circle and count the number of circles toward the outside edge until you reach the number in your plotting column, then place a dot at that point.

Plotting Key

A = Passive-Aggressive   B = Compulsive   C = Paranoid   D = Narcissistic   E = Codependent

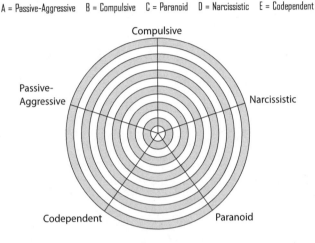

Figure 4

How Does Your Dark Side Influence Your Leadership?

0–4   Little to No Influence
4–8   Significant Negative Influence
8–12 Potentially Destructive Negative Influence

Once you have plotted all of your scores, you can connect the dots with straight lines to see more clearly where the largest influence of your dark side is located. The points farthest from the center of the circle indicate where your dark side has the most influence in your leadership.

NOTES

Preface

1. For a complete overview of the different generational groups in the church, see Gary L. McIntosh, *Three Generations: Riding the Waves of Change in Your Church* (Grand Rapids: Revell, 1995).

Introduction to the Revised Edition

1. *Leadership Journal* (Winter 2007): 97.
2. Erich Fromm, *To Have or to Be?* (Continuum: London, 1997), 13.
3. Ibid.
4. Ibid., 16.
5. C. G. Jung, *The Collected Works of C. G. Jung*, 2nd ed. (Princeton, NJ: Princeton University Press, 2000), 273.

Chapter 1 Blindsided by the Dark Side

1. Norman Shawchuck, *Leading the Congregations: Caring for Yourself While Serving the People* (Nashville: Abingdon, 1993), 94–95.

Chapter 2 Danger on the Dark Side

1. Traci Watson and Andrea Stone, "Attempted Murder Charge, Handcuffs Ground Astronaut," *USA Today*, February 7, 2007.
2. Ibid.
3. See Alex Prud'homme, *The Cell Game: Sam Waksal's Fast Money and False Promises—and the Fate of ImClone's Cancer Drug* (New York: HarperBusiness, 2004).

Chapter 3 Company on the Dark Side

1. Nathaniel Hawthorne, *The Scarlet Letter* (New York: Bantam, 1989), 128–34.

2. Chris Burbach and Julia McCord, "Omaha Pastor Charged with Exposing Himself," *Omaha World-Herald*, 31 May 1995, sec. B, p. 13.

3. Cindy Gonzalez, "Convicted Pastor Takes Sabbatical," *Omaha World-Herald*, 7 August 1995, sec. B, p. 11.

4. Charles E. Shepard, *Forgiven: The Rise and Fall of Jim Bakker and the PTL Ministry* (New York: Atlantic Monthly Press, 1989), 546.

5. Ibid., 547.

6. Jim Bakker's recent book reveals an attempt to get in touch with his dark side. Jim Bakker with Ken Abraham, *I Was Wrong* (Nashville: Thomas Nelson, 1996).

7. Lynne and Bill Hybels, *Rediscovering Church: The Story and Vision of Willow Creek Community Church* (Grand Rapids: Zondervan, 1995), 24.

8. Ibid., 106.

Chapter 4 Shedding Divine Light on the Dark Side

1. R. Laird Harris, Gleason L. Archer Jr., and Bruce K. Waltke, *Theological Wordbook of the Old Testament*, vol. 2 (Chicago: Moody, 1980), article 2121a, 833.

2. Warren Bennis, *On Becoming a Leader* (Reading, MA: Addison-Wesley, 1989), 45.

3. G. Ernest Wright, *Great People of the Bible and How They Lived* (Pleasantville, NY: Reader's Digest Association, 1974), 145.

4. The information recorded by Solomon in Ecclesiastes 2:1–11 seems to be consistent with the symptoms of narcissistic personality disorder (see chapter 9 for a definition of this personality disorder and a more complete discussion of this issue).

5. Exodus 18:13–27 indicates Moses felt a need to exhibit personal control over a vast number of people and a sense that he alone was capable of doing the job correctly. In addition, Moses' numerous public eruptions of anger would seem to indicate some repressed anger, possibly from his past failure in Egypt (see chapter 8 for a definition of this personality disorder and a more complete discussion of this issue).

Chapter 5 How the Dark Side Develops

1. Robert A. Johnson, *Owning Your Own Shadow: Understanding the Dark Side of the Psyche* (San Francisco: HarperSanFrancisco, 1991), 4.

2. Ibid.

3. Ralph G. Martin, *Seeds of Destruction: Joe Kennedy and His Sons* (New York: G. P. Putnam's Sons, 1995), xviii.

4. Ibid.

5. Ibid., 23.

6. Ibid., 373.

7. Ibid., 372.

8. Bernard Weiner, *Human Motivation* (Hillsdale, NJ: Lawrence Erlbaum Associates, 1980), 412.

9. James MacGregor Burns, *Leadership* (New York: Harper and Row, 1978), 79.

10. Ibid., 92.

11. Ibid., 91.

Chapter 7 Paradoxes of the Dark Side

1. PTL stood for "People That Love" during the early phases of that ministry and "Praise the Lord" during its final years.

2. Shepard, *Forgiven*, 30.

3. Ibid., 11.

4. Ibid., 18.

5. Ibid., 556.

6. Ibid., 559.

7. William Martin, *A Prophet with Honor: The Billy Graham Story* (New York: Quill, 1991), 74.

8. Ibid., 107.

Chapter 8 The Compulsive Leader

1. Careful readers of the Bible will note that Moses' mother and sister took an active interest in him during his early years (Exod. 2:4–9). He really was not abandoned but he may have at times felt abandoned. Adopted children often feel shunned, rejected, and disowned even though they may have a good relationship with both their adoptive and birth parents. Moses may have experienced similar feelings as a result of his unique childhood circumstances and upbringing.

2. Theodore Millon, *Disorders of Personality* (New York: John Wiley and Sons, 1981), 218.

3. Ibid., 225.

4. Ibid.

5. Ibid., 219.

6. Ibid., 227.

7. Ibid., 228.

Chapter 9 The Narcissistic Leader

1. Thomas Moore, *Care of the Soul: A Guide for Cultivating Depth and Sacredness in Everyday Life* (New York: Harper Perennial, 1992), 57–71.

2. Alexander Lowen, MD, *Narcissism: Denial of the True Self* (New York: Macmillan, 1983), 6.

3. Ibid.

4. Millon, *Disorders of Personality*, 159.

5. Shepard, *Forgiven*, 554.

Chapter 10 The Paranoid Leader

1. Millon, *Disorders of Personality*, 372.

2. Ibid., 373.

Chapter 11 The Codependent Leader

1. David Maraniss, *First in His Class: A Biography of Bill Clinton* (New York: Simon and Schuster, 1995), 30.
2. Ibid., 31.
3. Ibid., 32.
4. Ibid., 39–40.
5. Ibid., 38.
6. Paul M. Fick, *The Dysfunctional President: Inside the Mind of Bill Clinton* (New York: Carol Publishing, 1995), 42.
7. Ibid.
8. Ibid., 64.
9. Ibid., 67.
10. Ibid., 6.
11. Merrill F. Unger, *The New Unger's Bible Handbook* (Chicago: Moody, 1966), 97.
12. C. J. Goslinga, *Bible Student's Commentary: Joshua, Judges, Ruth* (Grand Rapids: Zondervan, 1986), 409.
13. Melody Beattie, *Codependent No More: How to Stop Controlling Others and Start Caring for Yourself* (San Francisco: HarperSanFrancisco, 1987), 32.
14. Ibid., 38.

Chapter 12 The Passive-Aggressive Leader

1. Millon, *Disorders of Personality*, 246.
2. John R. Lion, *Personality Disorders: Diagnosis and Management* (Baltimore: Williams and Wilkens, 1981), 587.
3. Millon, *Disorders of Personality*, 253.
4. Ibid., 246.
5. Ibid., 254.

Chapter 13 Overcoming the Dark Side

1. Donald T. Phillips, *Lincoln on Leadership: Executive Strategies for Tough Times* (New York: Warner, 1992), 80.
2. Ibid., emphasis ours.
3. Ibid., 81–82.
4. Ibid., 82.
5. Bennis, *On Becoming a Leader*, 69.

Chapter 14 Spiritual Composting

1. Judy Cannato, "The Compost Pile," *Weavings* 16, no. 1 (2001): 30.
2. Ibid.

Chapter 15 Step 1: Acknowledge Your Dark Side

1. "Fallen Clinton Advisor: Job Altered Reality," *Omaha World-Herald*, 24 November 1996, sec. A, p. 3.
2. Reported by Jeffrey Zaslow, "Straight Talk," *USA Weekend*, 7–9 February 1997, 18.

Chapter 16 Step 2: Examine the Past

1. Sue Grafton, quoted in Zaslow, "Straight Talk," 18.
2. Bennis, *On Becoming a Leader*, 64.
3. This is not to dismiss the possibility that an individual may have deeply repressed memories of traumatic, painful childhood events such as abuse of some sort that he or she subconsciously refuses to remember.
4. Bennis, *On Becoming a Leader*, 67.
5. Ibid., 61.
6. Neil Anderson, *Victory over the Darkness: Realizing the Power of Your Identity in Christ* (Ventura, CA: Regal, 1990), 201.
7. Ibid., 203–5.

Chapter 17 Step 3: Resist the Poison of Expectations

1. Robert L. Edmondson, *It Only Hurts on Monday: Why Pastors Quit and What Churches Can Do about It* (DMin diss., Talbot School of Theology, Biola University, December 1995), 111–12.
2. Ibid., 295.
3. Charles R. Swindoll, *The Grace Awakening* (Dallas: Word, 1990), 129.
4. Ibid., 132.

Chapter 18 Step 4: Practice Progressive Self-Knowledge

1. Anne Broyles, *Journaling: A Spirit Journey* (Nashville: The Upper Room, 1988), 13.
2. John Maxwell, personal interview, Denver, 17 May 1995.
3. Richard Dortch, "Blind Spot," *Leadership: A Practical Journal for Church Leaders XV*, no. 3 (summer 1994): 79.
4. Ibid., emphasis ours.
5. Ibid.

SUGGESTED READING LIST

For Further Study and Redemption of the Dark Side

Anderson, Neil T. *The Bondage Breaker*. Eugene, OR: Harvest House, 1990.

———. *Victory over the Darkness: Realizing the Power of Your Identity in Christ*. Ventura, CA: Regal, 1990.

Beattie, Melody. *Codependent No More: How to Stop Controlling Others and Start Caring for Yourself*. San Francisco: HarperSanFrancisco, 1987.

Bennis, Warren. *On Becoming a Leader*. Reading, MA: Addison-Wesley, 1989.

———. *Why Leaders Can't Lead: The Unconscious Conspiracy Continues*. San Francisco: Jossey-Bass, 1990.

Bennis, Warren, and Burt Nanus. *Leaders: The Strategies for Taking Charge*. New York: Harper and Row, 1985.

Blotnick, Srully. *Ambitious Men: Their Drives, Dreams and Delusions*. New York: Viking, 1987.

Burns, James MacGregor. *Leadership*. New York: Harper and Row, 1978.

De Pree, Max. *Leadership Is an Art*. New York: Dell, 1989.

Dortch, Richard. *Integrity: How I Lost It and My Journey Back*. Green Forest, AR: New Leaf, 1992.

Fick, Paul. *The Dysfunctional President: Inside the Mind of Bill Clinton*. New York: Carol Publishing, 1995.

Finzel, Hans. *The Top Ten Mistakes Leaders Make*. Wheaton, IL: Victor, 1994.

Ford, Leighton. *Transforming Leadership: Jesus' Way of Creating Vision, Shaping Values, and Empowering Change*. Downers Grove, IL: InterVarsity, 1991.

Hybels, Lynne and Bill. *Rediscovering Church*. Grand Rapids: Zondervan, 1995.

Kaplan, Robert E. *Beyond Ambition*. San Francisco: Jossey-Bass, 1991.

Kets de Vries, Manfred F. R., and Danny Miller. *The Neurotic Organization*. San Francisco: Jossey-Bass, 1984.

———. *Unstable at the Top: Inside the Troubled Organization*. New York: New American Library, 1987.

Kofodimos, Joan. *Balancing Act: How Managers Can Integrate Successful Careers and Fulfilling Personal Lives*. San Francisco: Jossey-Bass, 1993.

Kouzes, James M., and Barry Z. Posner. *Credibility: How Leaders Gain and Lose It, Why People Demand It*. San Francisco: Jossey-Bass, 1993.

Maraniss, David. *First in His Class: A Biography of Bill Clinton*. New York: Simon and Schuster, 1995.

Martin, Ralph G. *Seeds of Destruction: Joe Kennedy and His Sons*. New York: G. P. Putnam's Sons, 1995.

Martin, William. *A Prophet with Honor: The Billy Graham Story*. New York: Quill, 1991.

May, Gerald G., MD, *Addiction and Grace: Love and Spirituality in the Healing of Addictions*. San Francisco: HarperSanFrancisco, 1991.

McGee, Robert S. *The Search for Significance*. Houston: Rapha, 1990.

Phillips, Donald T. *Lincoln on Leadership: Executive Strategies for Tough Times*. New York: Warner, 1992.

Sanders, Oswald J. *Spiritual Leadership*. Chicago: Moody, 1967.

Schaef, Anne Wilson, and Diane Fassel. *The Addictive Organization*. San Francisco: Harper and Row, 1988.

Shawchuck, Norman, and Roger Heuser. *Leading the Congregations: Caring for Yourself while Serving the People*. Nashville: Abingdon, 1993.

Shepard, Charles E. *Forgiven: The Rise and Fall of Jim Bakker and the PTL Ministry*. New York: Atlantic Monthly, 1989.

Gary L. McIntosh (DMin, PhD) is president of the Church Growth Network and professor of Christian ministry and leadership at Talbot School of Theology. He is the author of several books, including *Biblical Church Growth* and *Beyond the First Visit*.

Gary speaks to numerous churches, organizations, schools, and conventions each year. He provides keynote presentations at major meetings, seminars and workshops, training courses, and ongoing consultation and coaching. For a live presentation of the material found in *Overcoming the Dark Side of Leadership*, or to request a catalog of materials or other information on Gary's availability and ministry, contact:

Church Growth Network
PO Box 892589
Temecula, CA 92589-2589
(951) 506-3086
Email: cgnet@earthlink.net
www.churchgrowthnetwork.com

Samuel D. Rima serves at Bethel Seminary in St. Paul, Minnesota, as the director of the Doctor of Ministry program and also on the faculty in the Center for Transformational Leadership. He has served as a church planter and senior pastor as well as a denominational executive with the Baptist General Conference. Sam holds a doctor of ministry degree in leadership and is currently a candidate for a PhD in spiritual and socioeconomic transformation from the University of Buckingham, United Kingdom. For resources to assist you in developing a personal plan for overcoming your dark side, as well as an online dark side profile for use with leadership teams and boards, visit www.samrima.com.

Also from **Gary L. McIntosh**
and **Samuel D. Rima**

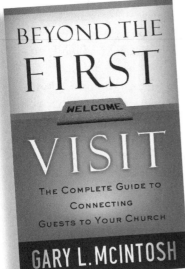

Beyond the First Visit:
The Complete Guide to Connecting Guests
to Your Church
By Gary L. McIntosh

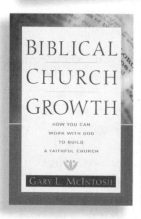

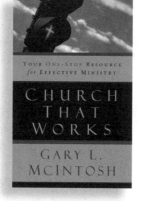

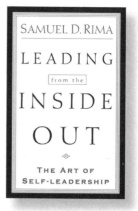

Biblical Church Growth:	**Church That Works:**	**Leading from the**
How You Can Work with God to	Your One-Stop Resource for	**Inside Out:**
Build a Faithful Church	Effective Ministry	The Art of Self-Leadership
By Gary L. McIntosh	By Gary L. McIntosh	By Samuel D. Rima

 BakerBooks
Relevant. Intelligent. Engaging. | a division of Baker Publishing Group | www.bakerbooks.com